Different Planets:

Understanding Your Neurodiverse Relationship

Different Planets:

Understanding Your Neurodiverse Relationship

by Lorna Hecker, Ph.D.

First Edition
Copyright © 2022 Lorna Hecker

First Printing, April 2022
All rights reserved.
Paperback ISBN: 978-1-64669-232-3
E-book ISBN: 978-1-64669-237-8

Table of Contents

DIFFERENT PLANETS. . .

8

Chapter 1:

Are We from Different Planets?

ND[1]: I've always felt like I am from a different planet. I watch people, study their behaviors, examine them. I try to act as normal as I can, but I know I am different. I've been aware from an early age that I did not fit in with society. My partner often says "Earth to Alex!" to catch my attention, as I can get deep in thought and it is hard to focus on anything else at that moment. I have trouble opening up to my partner, and they have a hard time understanding me anyway.

NT[2]: I might as well be speaking an alien language when I discuss my feelings with my partner. They never get it! I believe I am being as clear as I can be, but my partner does not seem to understand me. I feel lonely, isolated, and tired of taking care of all of the details in life. I'm burnt

---

[1] "Neurodivergent" or "neurodiverse," depending on context. A particular individual on the spectrum or having ADHD is considered "neurodivergent," but in a group of two or more people, "neurodiverse" is a term that applies when there are different brain styles represented in that group. So if one person is neurotypical and one is neurodivergent, they have a neurodiverse relationship.

[2] "Neurotypical;" not exhibiting ADHD, autism spectrum, or other atypical brain styles.

out, angry, and hurt. I am really unclear if they really care for me or not, or if I am just a mother figure. When we were first together, they were so attentive, but now I can hardly get any attention, let alone the feeling of love.

If you are in a relationship with someone who has a different brain style than yourself, it can feel like you are from different planets. You probably started your relationship thinking you understood the person, but over time, you realize you think very differently. These differences can appear in how you perceive the world, communicate, and express and receive love. Who, exactly, is this alien you live with? How can you be so different from each other?

These questions will begin to be answered in this book as we look at the role of neurodiversity in your relationship. Neurodiversity refers to variances in how we think, process information, reason, and understand the world. A neurodiverse relationship is when you and your partner have different brain styles. Neurodivergent refers to an individual who has cognitive functioning that differs significantly from what society deems as "normal" or "typical." They typically have been labeled as "disordered" by the mental health community, with labels such as Autism Spectrum *Disorder,* or ASD, (including Asperger's *Syndrome*) and Attention Deficit Hyperactivity *Disorder* (ADHD). Neurodivergence also includes learning impairments such as dyslexia (difficulties with reading), dysgraphia (difficulties with written expression), or dyscalculia (difficulties with math). Depending upon the source, those with Tourette's Syndrome and neurologically based mental health conditions such as OCD, bipolar, chronic anxiety or depression, and even PTSD may also considered neurodivergent.

> *Neurodivergent brain styles refers to people whose minds differ from what society deems as "normal" or "typical." For a neurodivergent individual, their brain style differs from the majority.*

What does it mean to be Neurodivergent or Neurotypical?

ND: Not only do I feel inside like I have an entirely different operating system, but when I put on clothes that other people typically wear, or wear devices like headphones, or even engage with other people, it feels odd. It looks wrong on me, but perfectly normal on other people. Like I'm cosplaying at being human, but with a low budget. I feel human when I'm by myself. When I'm around others I feel awkward and defective.

NT: I finally understand my partner just sees the world very differently than I do. It took me a long time, and my friends would wonder why I am with her, but I have come to appreciate that there are different ways to view things. I spent so much energy trying to convince her I was "right," and that most people would see things the way I do. I actually appreciate our differences now, but I had to grow and not think my view of the world was the "right" one. I appreciate the differences now rather than try to eradicate them.

A neurodivergent individual is someone who does not have "typical" neurological wiring; there is variation in neurocognitive functioning. It is a biological difference. When an individual diverges from what we consider "normal" neurocognitive functioning, they are *neurodivergent.* These differences in neurocognition can include areas that affect daily life such as attention, perception, language, learning and memory, "executive function" (this has to do with getting tasks done and will be discussed in Chapter 7), and social insight (APA, 2013).

Sociologist Judy Singer coined the term "neurodiversity" in 1998 and posited that neurodiversity is a normal human variation and those who are neurodiverse should be respected and accepted, rather than pathologized (2016). Others have put forth that this unique wiring brings many strengths that should be celebrated. One metaphorical way to view this is that those who are neurodiverse (ND) have a different computer operating system than our typical *Microsoft Windows,* for example, the lesser-known *Linux.* Getting these two systems to communicate with each other is a challenge for systems engineers. You are probably reading this book because you understand at an intimate level the feelings that go with this challenge of getting two different operating systems to communicate with each other! It can be frustrating, angering, or anguishing to attempt to communicate, and perhaps exhilarating and satisfying when it occurs!

In simpler terms, the wiring of the brains of neurodivergent individuals is different than "neurotypical" individuals. The result is that bridging the gap between two minds can be a challenge, especially as relationships mature, and patterns of distancing occur when two different brain styles colliding as couples traverse everyday life. As the examples indicate, this can lead to feeling misunderstood, alone, and isolated, especially when partners do not understand the impact of having different brain styles. A neurodiverse relationship may include neurotypical and neurodivergent living in tandem with each other or two neurodivergent individuals living together.

> *If someone is neurodivergent, they have different neurological wiring than what is "typical." Neurotypical means you have a similar brain style to the majority culture.*

"Neurotypical" means that an individual's neurocognitive functioning falls within what society views as "normal." This is a socially constructed norm, and many NTs believe that their partner should be the one to jump on their planet, the "normal" one, rather than finding a way to join orbits and appreciate the beauty of both planets. For example, those who are neurodivergent often pay great attention to detail, have superior analytical thinking, are keen observers, creative, and often passionate about their areas of interest. This, however, often gets lost as we race to understanding the "disorder" and overlook these endearing qualities, which were probably part of your initial attraction to your ND partner.

> *Neurotypical refers to the socially constructed norm that there is a neurologically normal pattern of cognitive functioning.*

Normality is a Social Construction

This movement towards neurodiversity as an alternative to the disability label has helped us focus on finding native strengths for those who are ND rather than focusing on correcting deficits and normalizing their behavior to fit the neurotypical ideal. Advocates say that normality is a socially constructed idea, and that ND individuals have been marginalized from a society that views them as abnormal because they are different. The movement maintains that there is not one type of "normal" brain; instead, there are different variations or brain styles, and they are all equally important, valid and useful in society. Temple Grandin is famous for saying "different, not less" (Grandin, 2020), which is an important distinction as we think about neurodiversity, and as you think about your partner. Your differences do not make one of you "less than," but you will be different from each other.

Advocates hope to move thinking away from disabilities to a society that celebrates neurodiversity. There is some controversy around the neurodiversity movement in that it is not uncommon for those who are neurodivergent to experience concerns that need attention or treatment. Parents of nonverbal autistic children, for example, take issue with the neurodiversity movement as it negates the challenges they face. I think both are true; we need to celebrate neurodiversity but understand that there are challenges for individuals who are neurodivergent living in a neurotypical world.

As this movement is occurring, there is also considerable variation in languaging and will continue to be as neurodivergent individuals find their rightful place in our society. As a warning, the languaging in this book may get quickly outdated as voices of the neurodivergent continue to express their preferences and outpace what has been printed in the existing literature, which to date is often written by neurotypicals "interpreting" for neurodivergent folks.

> *There is a movement to depathologize neurodivergent individuals and to normalize variations in brain styles, called the Neurodiversity Movement.*

Neurodiversity and the Revolt Against Ableism

ND: The thing that makes disabled people disabled is the society around them. Blind people must exist in a world run by visual-sensing people. Autistic people must exist in a world run by non-autistics.

NT: It irks me when I let people know my wife is on the autism spectrum, and they remark that she doesn't "look autistic." Even for myself, I had to learn how to check myself and not say things like "it's common sense" or "everybody knows this" when we are in arguments.

Part of the neurodiversity movement is a revolt against "ableism." Ableism is the view that able-bodied people or neurotypical people are the norm and fully human. People with different abilities or diversities are seen as less than or invisible. The false choice ND people face is to become "normal" or be ostracized; they are told that in order to be worthy they must learn to thrive in what feels like an oppressive environment. Neurodivergent individuals have also been referred to a "neurominorities," which captures the flavor that they are also normal, but their brain styles are in the minority.

> *Ableism is the view that only able-bodied people or neurologically typical people are fully human.*

ND=Neurodivergent, NT=Neurotypical

In this book, Neurodivergent individuals will be referred to as "ND," while Neurotypical individuals will be referred to as "NT." This book will focus a bit more closely on neurodiverse relationships that arise from neurodevelopmental disorders (Autism and/or ADHD) but will also resonate with the struggles of most neurodiverse relationships. Explanations from a human development lens, but the book is not meant to be interventive. That is, the impact of neurodiversity in the couple relationship is explored, but specific solutions are outside of the scope of this book. It is hoped that the understanding gained can help initiate healing of ailing neurodiverse relationships as well as enhance intimacy in already close neurodiverse relationships.

How Can Understanding Neurodiversity Help My Relationship?

ND: On good days, my wife marvels at my talents. She loves my energy and I make her laugh. On bad days, she lets me know that I am working at a dangerously below-average standard compared to all of her friend's husbands, and she blows up that I haven't emptied the dishwasher or remembered to feed the cat. I'm in a constant state of fight and flight, worried I might trigger her anger about something I forgot to do, or her frustration that she has to tell me what needs to be done.

NT: I married my partner after years of dating, adventures, and life transitions. Over time, though, a pattern developed where I felt stuck with more of the domestic labor. His ADHD would cause him to take on too many commitments, and it became a constant cycle of frustration. He is so talented, but struggles with schedules, paperwork, and being on time. I began to feel more like his mother than his partner, and we struggle with constant conflict over daily chores. It is exhausting.

If you are an ND individual, you may be frustrated with feeling misunderstood or blamed by your partner. It may feel like you are constantly walking through a mine field, not knowing what may cause your partner to react. Understanding yourself is key to understanding others, and it will be helpful to understand your own abilities as well as areas in which you may need assistance. This book can help explain some of the challenges you face in connecting with your NT partner. By understanding yourself, you can share this understanding with your partner, and they, too, can begin to understand the planet you inhabit. You can also learn to understand how your partner thinks, what is important to them, and why you have differences. This understanding can aid and enhance your relationship.

If you are NT person, you are likely frustrated trying to communicate with your ND partner. You may be tired of doing the *emotional labor* required to live with an ND partner. Emotional labor involves the work you do to keep those around you comfortable and happy (Hartley, 2018). You may be tired of your partner not understanding social rules and norms or embarrassed when they commit social faux pas. It can be particularly frustrating when you see your partner can be so brilliant in one area of life yet seemingly so inept in completing ordinary activities. This book will help you understand the origin of this frustration, put it into the context of neurodivergence, and begin to see your partner in a different light. This can aid both your understanding and communication and begin to join your orbits.

There are specific traits for those who are neurodivergent that may amplify common relationship problems and some that may be challenges specifically due to the neurodiversity itself. There are also specific responses that are common to NT partners who don't understand the neurodiversity that amplifies relationship problems. This sets couples off on relational dances where intimacy can get lost and misunderstandings flourish.

Wait, what if *both* of us are ND? Yes, many folks who are ND pair up and go on to have successful relationships. This book can also help you understand each other. Knowledge is the key to understanding!

> *Understanding the impact of neurodiversity on your relationship can aid in couple understanding, communication, and connection.*

Why I Wrote this Book

I wrote this book because, after both teaching marriage and family therapy for 25 years and being a licensed marriage and family therapist seeing couples in my practice, I noticed neurodiverse couples did not respond to "typical" treatment. Many complained they had been to traditional couple's therapy, and it didn't work.

Neurodivergent spouses often got maligned due to their difficulty in understanding their partner's feelings and failing to respond in a neurotypical way to a likely neurotypical therapist. As they described their therapy, I would notice hints of a subtle (or overt) alliance between the neurotypical spouse and the neurotypical therapist, with frustration that the neurdivergent spouse would just not "get" what they were talking about. In all of the literature available in my career teaching marriage and family therapy, there wasn't anything that addressed the dynamics of neurodiverse couples. It was as if they didn't exist.

The methods of couple's therapy I had learned, taught, and used did not meet the needs of neurodiverse couples. Traditional couple's therapy is designed for neurotypical spouses and is often feelings-focused, which is a neurotypical need and often not a first language for someone who is neurodivergent. It does not take into account brain-style differences, and the models themselves disadvantage a neurodivergent spouse. I thought if I, as a professional therapist, do not have these resources, what about my clients? How can they begin to understand what is going on for them in relation to each other? This book was born as a way to normalize neurodiverse relationships, to invite readers to understand each other, and to shed light on a topic that has been sorely overlooked.

> *Typical couple therapy does not adequately address the role of neurodiversity and leaves the ND partner feelings pathologized and the NT partner feeling dissatisfied that their partner does not respond in a "neurotypical" way.*

Overlapping Brain Styles

During the development of this book, some of my gracious couple's-therapy clients read it. In one heterosexual couple, they began to understand the husband was on the autism spectrum, but he had never been formally diagnosed. As they read the book, his wife said to me, "Hey, am I neurodivergent too? Some of the neurodivergent things fit for me too. . ." She had some PTSD she was dealing with due to early-childhood abuse. I reminded her that PTSD also brings forward some ND traits, as she often found herself being reactive to her husband for no discernable reason.

In my experience, NT spouses who have been traumatized early in life gravitate to the reliability and predictability of an ND spouse. ND folks tend to be regimented, stick to routines, and be knowledgeable and morally grounded. This initially attracts someone who has had a chaotic upbringing or faced traumatic events as children, but as the relationship progresses, the NT spouse learns that they have traded stability needs for intimacy needs. As the relationship matures, they realize that their partner is harder to connect to on an emotional level, and they experience a loss as they realize they feel alone in their relationship. This is often when the challenges begin for the couple as they learn how to navigate these differences in expectation of intimacy. At this point they may reach out for some help to understand why closeness has become elusive when they once felt comfortable and connected. It is typically the neurotypical spouse who rings the alarm bell that there is intimacy lacking in the relationship, but both partners may feel like they have floated into "roommate" status. This drifting may occur if the couple does not engage in conflict and do not resolve issues, but it also may occur if conflict has been hazardous and nonproductive.

Conversely, ND spouses often find that their partner initially marveled at their abilities, enjoyed their idiosyncrasies, and "got" them in ways others did not. They felt accepted and safe to be themselves. As this safety grew, they became more comfortable with being who they are, only to find their partner complaining that they are distant and not putting the energy into the relationship as they once did. The criticism grows, and with each interaction, what was once a safe haven becomes a jarring experience on the nervous system, activating the fight-flight-or-freeze response. The nervous system's response to potential threat causes the ND person to withdraw, further threatening reliability and safety of the relationship for the NT person, who often responds with more of the same (elevated requests, threats, or demands).

Pursuer-Distancer Couple Pattern

This pattern often plays out within the couple relationship as a classic "pursuer-distancer" relationship as the dance of intimacy occurs. It may start with the NT partner complaining about their intimacy needs not being met, but often this comes out, or is received by the ND partner as criticism. The criticism shuts down the ND partner, who typically has a more sensitive nervous system attuned to threat, and they often withdraw (perhaps first responding with their own anger/criticism). This withdrawal is further experienced as abandonment, dismissal or disrespect by the NT partner, who further complains, and the cycle continues to the point both partners are frustrated and distanced. The NT partner feels justified in their complaining, buttressing their argument by aligning with the neurotypical majority by saying things like "anyone else would understand this" or "you are the only person who doesn't get this!"

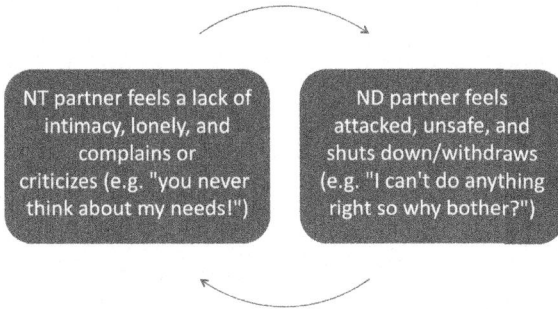

Figure 1.

This pattern (as seen in Figure 1) is typically what lands a couple in trouble as they have a hard time disengaging from their stuck positions in the relationship. Each see their partner as the "cause" of the problem, and life would be grand, if only the *other* person would change! This pattern can change as partners begin to understand why they are engaging in these positions (unmet needs), can gain some perspective on what is happening, and begin to discuss their needs in a more productive manner. This is often easier said than done, and it can take some time to break these relational patterns, especially if they have been long-standing patterns of interaction. Sometimes just a "look" can start the pattern rolling! This book will help you recognize these patterns so you can begin to find more satisfying ways of relating to each other.

Diversity within Neurodiversity

This book is based on information from human development, in an effort to educate neurodiverse couples on how developmental differences experienced by the ND partner may be affecting their relationship. It is not based on science of neurodiverse relationships, as we simply do not have a research base for neurodiverse couples, yet. This book is also not chock full of advice; rather, the goal is to illustrate how neurodiversity may be woven into the fabric of your relationship so that you can better understand your interactions and connection (or in some cases, disconnection).

Neurodiversity is, well. . . diverse! Some of what is in this book may apply perfectly to you or your relationship, but some of it may not. It is not a "one size fits all" book; take what is useful to you, and know that what doesn't fit you, may fit someone else reading this book. There are many types of neurodivergence and within each type significant variations. However, you may find yourself or your relationship within these pages. Patterns develop when ND and NT individuals are in intimate relationships; this book simply points out some of the common patterns that develop based on this interaction.

This book also illustrates intimate thoughts of neurodiverse people that were largely gathered or adapted from publicly available threads on discussion forums, to which access was not restricted in any way. Information has been treated with care to not reveal identities or specific characteristics of any individual.

Lastly, this book renders information that is likely not useful to individuals requiring very substantial support where there are severe deficits in both verbal and nonverbal social communication skills.

Why in the World Should I Read this Book?

If you are a neurotypical individual in a relationship with a neurodivergent person, you need to understand how they think differently than you. It is very common to pathologize that which is different, rather than appreciate the beauty that can lie within the differences. If you remember back to when you first met your partner, it was likely this difference that actually attracted you to them. This book can help you understand that difference, and aid you in both increasing your understanding of your partner, and decreasing your frustration with things that often have neurological underpinnings. It is often a big relief to know that your partner is not intentionally trying to upset, anger, or distance from you. I encourage you to think about what it would be liked to be dropped on a planet where you do not know the language, customs, and social rules. How would you feel?

If you are a neurodivergent person, you too will benefit from understanding that you and your partner are from different worlds, and that you need to engage in some cross-cultural understanding so you both feel the type of closeness you need to sustain a relationship. While understanding each other will not solve all problems, it can greatly increase acceptance, trust, and enhance connection in relationships. While there may be some disabling aspects of your neurodiversity, this book can also bring an appreciation of the many strengths that come from being different from the norm. This book should help you feel that even if you *do* come from different planets (metaphorically speaking) you can join orbits and be on the same trajectory!

Chapter 2:

Sharing Life When in Different Orbits

The most common issue neurodiverse couples bring to therapy centers around not feeling connected. This charge is often led by the NT partner, and they often are the ones to call for therapy, or if they are extremely frustrated, they have their ND spouse call because they are "tired of doing everything." These couples have gotten out of mutual orbit, and are frustrated by the lack of connection or the conflict they encounter just trying to do daily life. There are some neurodevelopmental differences that have contributed to this lack of connection, and in this chapter we will look at developmental concepts *Joint Attention* and *Theory of Mind* that typically differ for those who are ND.

Joint Attention

> *ND: I just want someone who thinks that supposedly "boring" and "complex" technical information is as fascinating as I do! My spouse asked me how my day was, and I had to "dumb it down" to one rudimentary sentence they could understand. I feel so lonely.*

> *NT: My girlfriend has trouble carrying on conversations. She will monologue for upwards of ten minutes without missing a beat, but tunes out as soon as I start to talk. It is so frustrating!*

Sharing in relationships requires what has been termed by developmental psychologists as "joint attention." This means that conversational partners focus and discuss one thing of interest to both parties. When we are babies, this means we learn to follow a parent's gaze or pointing finger to look at something. As we grow older, this gets accompanied with language. There is generally a reciprocal give-and-take in conversation as one topic is focused on. Joint attention helps us with sharing intentions, thoughts, memories, observations, and experiences with others, and this helps regulate closeness and distance in relationships (Caruana, et al., 2018).

In couple relationships, we bid for attention from our spouse numerous times throughout the day. Marital researcher John Gottman (2004, 2015) notes that we make bids from our partner for attention, acceptance, or support. It is the adult version of "will you play with me?" As couples turn towards each other in everyday bids for connection, they build what Gottman terms your "emotional bank account." The larger this bank account balance is, the easier it typically is to navigate conflict. Unfortunately, these difficulties maintaining joint attention for the ND person often result in frustration for the NT partner. When the ND partner has a hard time focusing on the activities or concerns of the NT partner, the NT partner may believe their partner does not care for them enough to be interested in their life. This can cause distance over time, as the ND partner delves enthusiastically into their own interests, but leaves their NT partner feeling they do not care about theirs. This causes a connection breach, and can grow if not addressed in a timely manner.

This can be frustrating as the couple starts out with common interests and activities in the beginning of their relationship, only to find themselves drifting away from each other over time. Typically, the ND partner tends not to notice this as readily since they may be engaging in their own interests, but it is the NT partner who rings the alarm bell that they are "not doing anything together anymore." They may understand their partner is not happy, but not understand why. The NT partner may start to build a separate life in order to get intimacy needs met, and depending upon how this is done, can positively or negatively affect the relationship.

Developmentally, ND individuals often have difficulty with establishing and maintaining joint attention, which helps regulate closeness and distance within relationships. They do well if there are shared common interests but may have difficulty feigning interest in things that their partners are interested in that they are not.

Birthdays, Anniversaries and Other Disasters

ND: I struggle significantly with remembering things like dates (especially birthdays and anniversaries). Birthdays and other traditional events are as meaningless to me as small talk. I have trouble remembering exactly when my partner's birthday is and getting a gift in advance. Should I get presents year round to compensate for forgetting?

NT: This is the second year he forgot my birthday. He said he would put it in his phone so he wouldn't forget. I'm trying not to be childish about this, but my birthday is important to me!

27

Special events require planning, which may tap into executive functioning deficits of an ND partner. "Executive functioning" refers to cognitive processes including organizing, planning, and scheduling and will be discussed further in Chapter 7. Difficulties with these cognitive processes often leaves the NT partner in charge of things such as remembering birthdays, anniversaries, holidays, and organizing family visits. It is not unusual for these types of events to be friction points in neurodiverse relationships. The ND partner can feel nervous, noting these events become "tests" they must pass in order to show adequate caring for the spouse. The NT partner often feels so overburdened with managing the executive functioning tasks of daily life, that they often secretly hope their partner recognizes their hard work and rewards them appropriately on their special day. They are looking for a reciprocity for their hard work of planning, organizing, or managing tasks and will more likely interpret failures on these special days as lack of caring. Special days can inadvertently turn into dreaded events, based on this pattern. Some partners deal with this in a self-defensive way by saying that the events are unimportant to them, which may temporarily fend off some hurt, but is not a good-long term strategy, as resentments can build and simmer.

This means that the NT partner may be the one remembering birthdays, but they may not have theirs remembered. The importance of noting an anniversary may be overlooked. Or the NT partner may understand exactly what their partner would enjoy as a gift, but their ND partner has no clue about what a meaningful gift for them would be. One of the building blocks of relationships is what marital researcher John Gottman (2004;2015) calls "love maps." Love maps are where you store information about your partner, what they like, what they dislike, what their hopes and dreams are, and so on. These maps need continual updating in order to stay relevant. For example, your favorite food may change over time. Because of the difficulties with emotional reciprocity, love maps can be a challenge to maintain for the ND spouse. The ND partner may assume that what they like is what their partner would like for a gift only to be baffled when they find their partner is angry or disappointed.

This can be particularly frustrating for the NT partner when they see their ND spouse remembering all sorts of facts, figures, and obscure information. However, how we encode "relevant" data varies by person, and for the ND person, what is interesting to them (for example, historical facts and figures) may be easily remembered while the more routine realm of birthdays or anniversaries do not rise to the same level of interest. For those on the autism spectrum, there is evidence that they have difficulty remembering social information compared to nonsocial facts (Boucher & Bowler 2008); adults with ADHD also have memory deficits reflecting a learning deficit induced at the stage of encoding the memory (Skodzik, Holling, & Pedersen, 2017). Again, these differences then tend to get pathologized not only by the NT spouse, but also by society, potentially leaving the ND person feeling like a failure.

Combine this difficulty with emotional reciprocity and deficits in executive functioning, then add in memory deficits, and it can be a perfect recipe for making special days seem like dreaded nightmares for both parties!

> *Birthdays, anniversaries and other important events can seem like emotional quicksand that cause couples to feel frustrated. NT partners often feel underappreciated and want recognition of these important events; for ND partners, it can feel like a minefield when there are executive functioning issues required such as planning and executing special events. What can look like lack of caring when important events are overlooked is often due to difficulties with both emotional reciprocity and executive function issues such as planning, organizing, and managing tasks.*

Emotional Reciprocity

ND: I am not a sociopath. I feel joy, I feel sadness, I feel love. I care very much about friends and family, want to support them, and I try hard to be a good person. I am devastated when I lose important people in my life. I have to think outside the box to feel empathy, though; it doesn't come naturally. I am very self-centered, and in my relationship there is always conflict. I just can't put myself in my partner's shoes until long after the fact.

NT: My boyfriend is on the spectrum and I am neurotypical. He gets so disproportionally upset with me for human error. At first, I thought he didn't care when he was making me cry, but I realized he didn't understand that his anger was causing me to cry. I would ask, "Can you tell

*me why you think I'm upset right now?" and he didn't un-
derstand, he was so focused on his anger. I realize I've been
expecting him to act and react neurotypically, and then
I've been confused when he doesn't.*

The recognition of the emotional states of others is often challenging for those who are neurodivergent. Emotional recognition
requires integrating cues from various channels such as facial expressions, vocal intonation, body language, and an understanding
of contextual information. For these reasons, those who are ND
can find it challenging to read others, which can contribute to social anxiety. Within the context of the couple relationship, they
may be able to make some good guesses about the thoughts and
feelings of their partner but are at a loss to understand
him/her/them on a consistent basis. What also can happen is that
the ND partner has spent so much energy masking and getting
through the day, they have less bandwidth for reflecting on their
partner's life. This does not mean an ND partner does not have
emotion; many actually have an uncomfortable level of empathy.
However, how they express this may be different or difficult to de-
tect. Difficulties in this area leave the NT partner missing the
feeling of connection that comes when your partner just "gets
you."

This should not be confused with thinking that the ND person lacks emotions; this is simply not true. What is true is they
have difficulty understanding and *expressing* those emotions.

It is not uncommon for this lack of emotional reciprocity to
earn the ND partner the label of "narcissistic." However, narcissism typically also involves a desire to be the center of attention;
most ND folks shun being the center of attention due to social
anxiety. While narcissism and ND are not necessarily mutually
exclusive, oftentimes it is the lack of emotional reciprocity that
causes that label, not true narcissism.

> ND persons can have difficulty reading the emotions of others, leading the NT partner to feel misunderstood or even alone. Likewise, ND individuals can get confused in emotional terrain if their partners are not transparent with their feelings and clearly communicating them.

Theory of Mind

ND: Having Asperger's or ADHD feels like trying to act in a play, where everyone else has the script except you, and then they get mad at you for improvising.

NT: I am just starting to realize how the issues my long-term partner and I struggle with are the result of him not understanding how my brain works and me not understanding how his brain works. He can be very closed off and stubborn and too much emotional conversation can overwhelm him.

Theory of Mind refers to the ability to attribute mental states (for example, beliefs, intents, feelings, actions) to oneself or someone else. It means that we understand that others have beliefs, desires, and perspectives that are different from our own. It allows us to analyze, judge, and infer from others' behaviors. There is a general awareness both of ourselves and of others (Astington & Edward, 2017). *Some* neurodiverse individuals lack Theory of Mind, but not all (Gernsbacher & Yergeau, 2019); this varies just as it does in the neurotypical population. Sometimes, an ND partner may have spent a good deal of time thinking about how their partner thinks but does not communicate their perception, leaving the NT feeling that their partner does not know them.

32

Other times, there is a lack of connection due to limited Theory of Mind.

For the NT partner, this lack of communicated understanding by their partner can be frustrating, and at times, they can feel their own reality is being denied when little about their lives is reflected back to them by their partner. Additionally, many ND partners have stellar logic and can argue logical points with insistence and even enjoyment to the point the NT partner gets exhausted trying to defend their view of reality. It may undermine the NT person's self-confidence, and they can feel invalidated by their partner. This is typically due to a mismatch in expectations. The ND partner is looking to understand where their partner is by understanding their thought process, while the NT partner is typically looking to be understood by having their feelings understood. This mismatch can leave both partners exasperated.

For the ND partner, if there is limited Theory of Mind, it can be very difficult to see their partner's point of view. They will argue their view is the "right" one and do not understand the upset or anger they cause at presenting this "right" view. Surely everyone wants to get at the truth, which they are kindly providing! This skill of taking the perspective of another person is typically underdeveloped due to neurological differences and causes consternation for the ND person when they cannot predict how their spouse will react. It feeds into a feeling of "walking on eggshells" as they often do not know what is going to "set their partner off." They may say things that seem insensitive and or are downright hurtful. Without clarifying communication, this dynamic can cause damage to their relationship. The NT partner may have to say "that really hurt my feelings when you said (fill in the blank)," to alert the ND partner that their communication has gone astray.

These differences in Theory of Mind can bring never-ending cycles of conflict if not understood. NT folks typically again expect their partner to have a map of their emotional life and be able

33

to reflect that in couple communication. One ND spouse explained their arguments in the following way: "I think the purpose of arguing is that we can learn from each other. If one of us is 'more right' than the other, then the person who is 'less right' can become 'more right.' To me, closeness occurs if I trust someone enough to be corrected by them." By not understanding the ND Theory of Mind, especially in understanding conflict, we are limited in understanding how to bridge two worlds.

> *Theory of Mind refers to our ability to understand the beliefs, intents, feelings, and actions of others when they are different from our own. Both partners can suffer from underdeveloped Theories of Mind. ND partners may have difficulty understanding that their partner's views are different from their own; NT partners may be unable to understand differences in how their partner thinks, especially how they view the purpose of conflict.*

Chapter 3:

Hyperfocus and Special Interests. . . Superpowers or Kryptonite?

Neurodivergent individuals typically have two stellar characteristics that stand out to others: hyperfocus and specialized interests, which go hand in hand. These can be great strengths; in fact, these areas where the ND partner shines may have been what initially attracted their partner to them. At the same time, these seeming superpowers can cause some tensions in couple relationships as they are navigated.

Hyperfocus

ND: The good thing is my professional life is thriving because it is aligned with my special interest, on which I love to focus. While I excel in the area I hyperfocus on, everyone and everything else gets neglected in the bargain, be it children, pets, bill payments, even my own health. I'm tired of disappointing others. I often miss what my husband says to me when I'm in the middle of doing something else and he is getting upset that I'm ignoring him.

It's not intentional on my part, but it's like I will hear what he says and it will register way later that something even happened.

NT: My wife was so focused on me when we first met, and it really hurt when this just seemed to fall off. She assures me she still cares, but I miss the intensity we had, and it is hard not to take it personally. I feel confused and unimportant, and getting her to listen to me is a real challenge these days. I just feel so lonely most days.

ND persons often have an superior ability to hyperfocus on the interest at hand. Hyperfocus occurs when one gets completely absorbed in a task that one finds fun or interesting, effectively tuning out everything else (Ashinoff & Abu-Akel, 2019). What often attracts NTs to NDs is often their amazing ability to hyperfocus, to have or develop expertise in a specific area and excel. They can be remarkable, interesting, and intriguing individuals! There is evidence that hyperfocus occurs more frequently in those with the neurodevelopmental disorders of Autism and ADHD (Ashinoff & Abu-Akel, 2019).

In response to their spouse's intense specialized interests, NT partners may get frustrated trying to get their partner back on the planet when they need them. Ordinary human needs get shuffled to the side as the laser focus of the ND partner has captured them, with a return-to-earth date that is unknown to all. NTs initially see some of this absorption into topics as "eccentricities," but over time, the extended difficulty in connecting, as well as feeling deprioritized, starts to tarnish this initial luster. NT partners often complain "I am often last on their list of priorities."

> *The amazing hyperfocus abilities of an ND partner can leave the NT spouse feeling neglected or ignored. Most people report that when their ND partner is hyperfocused, there is little they can do to get them rooted back in the present moment.*

Specialized Interests

ND: I have a special interest in anatomy and physiology, which works well in my professional (medical) world, but I think about it all the time. I can't communicate with anyone without bringing up something medical-related, and I have a hard time recognizing when I am asking questions that are too personal. I can't really explain where my specialized interest came from or why I love it; I just do. I just have a hard time doing or thinking about anything else.

*NT: I really am proud of how my spouse has excelled in their career. Yet, I often find I feel disappointed that they would rather spend time working than be with me. It is hard to have conversations about things **other** than their job. I just really want more depth in our relationship!*

ND individuals are known to develop specialized interests or topics about which they become experts. The range of potential specialized interests is as wide as the universe. A high tolerance for solitude combined with hyperfocus is a recipe for developing amazing specialized interests. When an ND person can align a career with specialized interests, they can excel tremendously. Unless their NT partner shares this specialized interest, it can feed the problem of lack of joint attention, leaving their partner feeling like their needs come after the specialized interest. This is not typically the intent of the ND person, but is a byproduct of their brain style. The fixations on specialized interests for the ND person can feel compulsive, as opposed to hobbies of NTs that seem to be more of a conscious choice. Hyperfocus can be a double-edged sword for the ND person as it can bring extensive expertise but less connection with others who do not share the specialized interest.

When ND individuals meet their partners, they may even make the partner one of their "special interests" and be completely absorbed in them. However, over time, this interest changes as attention wanes, leaving the NT partner feeling cheated or tricked. There is a longing for the days they were made to feel special by their partner.

Not everyone develops special interests, though, and stereotypes that arise from pop culture can also do damage. If we expect every neurodivergent person to perform at the level of Temple Grandin, Einstein, or Bill Gates, it discounts the level of struggle that many NDs face living in an NT world.

> *While not universal, many ND persons can develop significant specialized interests. Unless these are shared interests, the NT partner can feel ignored or rejected when the ND partner invests significant time and energy in their specialized interests but may appear to have little energy or interest in their life partner over time.*

Chapter 4:

Making Contact: Differences in Receptive and Expressive Language

ND: It seems I just can't get it right or find the perfect formula for communication. When I think I am saying one thing, my wife thinks I am saying something completely different. It can be so frustrating. My wife struggles with my lack of emotion in language, and the fact that I keep the same face regardless of what we speak. She interprets this as disinterest, annoyance, or anger. How can I help her understand I make the same face regardless? Sometimes I try to make a joke and she takes it seriously because she says my face looks "angry." I've asked her to check in with me, but she is uncomfortable being so blunt, which I need.

NT: My husband has a brilliant engineering career, but constantly has trouble at work with colleagues. He struggles with office politics and interactions with coworkers. His evaluations suffer even though I am convinced he is the smartest person there. Even I have a hard time understanding where he is coming from sometimes. I often ask if he is angry, but he almost always denies he is angry, in spite of his facial expression. I feel constantly confused and frustrated trying to understand him.

Receptive language means you have the ability to understand what others say or what you read. Expressive language is about being able to put your thoughts into words. You can think of it as "input" and "output." Both the input (what you take in from the outside world) and output (what you express to the outside world) can be very different for the ND person than the NT person. This can make for delightful differences, outside-the-box thinking, and creativity, but within relationships, can also lead to major misunderstandings.

It is not that NT people are perfect communicators just because they are NT people. NT people live in a NT world and interpret the world through that lens. Part of what an ND partner may face is difficulties in expression or understanding that are different than the experience of most NT people. NT people, through their own receptive wiring, interpret facial expressions but, much to the dismay of the ND partner, will interpret the ND partner from this same lens that does not fit for the ND partner. In not understanding their brain differences, the NT partner may label their ND partner as having "inappropriate" reactions or facial expressions. As in our example above, their partner may get negative feedback at work about this as well, further bolstering the NT person's argument that something is wrong with them, or they need to change.

Imagine if roles were reversed, and NTs lived on a planet where the majority of people had limited facial expressions and body language. NTs would have a hard time functioning because they would be missing the clues needed to understand those around them. The ND population would be relying largely on language, leaving the NTs searching for facial expressions and body language. When the COVID pandemic hit, this actually did occur for many psychotherapists, who were used to being able to get additional information from body language, respiration, facial cues; we were left searching for these cues via our Zoom screens, and many complained of how exhausting it was. In corporate America, many resorted to turning their cameras off in meetings as they found paying attention to all the stimuli too exhausting.

If an ND person is asked to make certain facial expressions, they will likely feel like inauthentic clowns. It is not normal nor natural for them. Additionally, for some, they may be able to focus on facial expressions or content, but both may be too much stimulation to manage.

Literal Interpretations

ND: If my partner says "I'll be home after lunch," I don't know exactly when "lunch" is and I don't know how long they consider "after" to be. Saying "I'll be with you some time between 12 and 1, I'll text you when I leave home" is so much better. I'd argue neurotypicals are the challenged ones, always mincing their words and thinking you mean something other than what you are telling them to their face!

NT: My partner takes instructions very literally. If I say, "please put the groceries away," she will put the groceries away, and leave the bags on the counter, because I didn't add "and dispose of the bags afterwards." While I have a good sense of humor, my sarcasm often goes over her head; my sarcastic tone does not seem to register and she completely misses what I think is hilarious.

In typical communication, our facial cues tell others when we are being sarcastic or we don't mean something literally. This may also be accompanied by a certain voice inflection so the other person knows not to take us literally. ND folks often have difficulty with figurative language, so they tend to take things literally. They may not understand the "unspoken" or "hidden" parts of language,

41

and they sometimes miss the emotion behind the language if someone is happy or angry, for example. They often have difficulty "reading" the faces of others, even when the other person thinks they are being obvious with their nonverbals. The ND individual will pick up on *what* was said but may miss *how* it was said, as well as the underlying messages that lie in the nonverbal communication.

Language always has two levels of meaning: the denotative meaning (what is said) and the connotative meaning (what is meant). Think of how many ways the answer of "I'm fine" in response to "How are you?" can be interpreted! The sender could be giving a cheery, melodic "I'm fine," or it could be a sarcastic "I'm fine!", and there are literally hundreds of other meanings for just these two words.

ND folks tend to focus only on the denotative meaning, missing the connotative meaning, much to the chagrin of their partners. For example, one woman complained that her boyfriend gave her a pair of earrings for her birthday. They both agreed they were lovely and she thanked him and was pleased he remembered her so nicely. However, in the course of conversation, she found out that he had actually bought the earrings for his ex-wife but had never gotten around to giving them to her before they divorced. An argument ensued where the girlfriend was incensed that her beau did not understand how this was insulting, and he did not understand why she did not appreciate the lovely earrings. A stalemate occurred where she felt unappreciated, and he was left baffled and thought she was a bit selfish.

In this case of the boyfriend giving his girlfriend earrings he had bought for his ex-wife, the denotative meaning is "a pair of lovely earrings" that both partners agreed were nice. However, he missed the connotative meaning that his girlfriend would not feel special because the earrings were originally intended for someone else.

This difficulty with connotative meaning may cause the ND partner to have troubles with idioms ("it is raining cats and dogs"), metaphors ("you are my sunshine"), similes ("crazy like a fox"), and irony (a police station has a robbery). Difficulties with understanding connotative meaning can leave the NT partner feeling misunderstood or like they cannot share life's humor, and the ND partner may have difficulty laughing at themselves or understanding jokes, irony, or sarcasm. Typical couple banter may get truncated due to frustrations in understanding each other.

Not understanding when someone is *using* sarcasm is not the same as not understanding it. There are certain cues we put out when we use sarcasm. For example, our tone of voice or facial expression typically telegraph sarcasm to the listener. These cues may be initially missed by the ND partner, but once the context is provided and the switch in mindset is made, the ND person can readily enjoy it. Neurodivergent folks are seldom a dull lot. They often excel at puns, wordplay, and language-based jokes and become masters at sarcasm, deadpans, and one-liners.

Understanding Social Rules

ND: My wife describes herself as my social interpreter. She understands that I don't like social events but helps me get through them. She provides the social excuses when she sees I have hit my limit and need to leave an event.

NT: I have difficulties with the monologues. A conversation that should take less than a minute can take hours! I'm either bored or frustrated and don't know how to get him to stop doing this. He gets mad if I interrupt his train of thought. I end up feeling trapped, he will get mad if I leave, but if I stay, I am bored to death.

ND individuals typically have difficulty reading and interpreting body language and facial expression. Couple this with the invisible social rules in the NT world when the ND person is relying on literal interpretation, and they can feel completely lost in social contexts. NT individuals often learn about social rules intuitively, while for ND individuals it is an active, cognitive process they must work at. NDs have to actively think through what has worked in the past and what hasn't. Additionally, ND individuals will mostly receive feedback when they make a mistake (and are rarely rewarded for interpreting correctly), which can lead to increased anxiety and decreased self-confidence about social interactions. Additionally, ND persons have typically had a litany of social interactions that have been traumatic. If you have had numerous negative interactions in daily life, you will naturally tend to shy away from others, cleaving to the safety of introversion. They are often steeped in social anxiety because of these difficulties. Additionally, many ND clients tell me they agonize over social interactions and "replay" previous social interactions in their heads over and over again, castigating themselves for how they reacted.

It's not unusual to hear from the NT spouse, "But I am their only friend!" Making and keeping friends with limited social skills can be challenging. Pair that with the downtime needed to recuperate from social interaction needed for work or school, and space for friends becomes limited. Then add in the bullying that many ND individuals have experienced in their earlier life, and the wall to climb to get friends can seem unreasonably high. The ND individual will feel like they have spent most of their life as an outcast and often say something like "I just feel like an outsider looking in" on social situations. Some grow comfortable with this more reclusive role in life; others remain uncomfortable in their own skin, constantly wrestling with an internal message that says "There is something fundamentally wrong with me."

It is also possible that ND individuals do get social cues, but often times NT individuals give inauthentic social cues. There are numerous things NTs do that make no sense to an ND person.

Fake smiles, sarcastic comments, indirect hints, and so on can be extremely confusing for an ND person. Perhaps if NT folks were more authentic in their communication, ND folks would not be so confused! In other words, if you actually mean what you say, it would be much easier for your ND partner.

> *ND individuals learn social skills cognitively, rather than intuitively; it takes a lot of work to understand others. NT folks tend to be indirect and often do not say what they mean in a clear way, further causing difficulties in communication between partners.*

Alien Small Talk

ND: You know, black holes and aliens and shit are interesting. Small talk, in my opinion, sucks eggs.

NT: I've tried every communication trick I know, but they say "I don't feel like talking" or "I have nothing to say."

Small talk is typically about unimportant matters, and in the neurotypical world, we use this type of conversation as a first step in relationships. It helps us gauge whether or not we want to get closer to a person. It is typically seen as polite to engage in small talk. Relationships normally progress from small talk to casual acquaintances to casual friends, and we may then move to close friends or intimate friends. Small talk provides the gateway to closeness. It is a social ritual with this purpose in mind. For NTs, the content of small talk is not the issue; the issue is the desire to connect.

However, for ND individuals, this process works differently. ND individuals connect to ideas or intellectual content. If this

45

content is something that they find engaging, NDs will connect with the other person around the ideas/content. This is an important distinction: for NT individuals this initial discussion of meaningless content leads to connection, which leads to deeper discussion of shared content. However, for ND individuals, there is little interest in meaningless content. For ND individuals shared content leads to connection. Thus we have different planets. . . NTs start with meaningless content (small talk) to get to connection; NDs start with meaningful content (to them) to get to connection.

For NDs, then, small talk is a form of masking and is energy-draining (and many of us NTs also don't like small talk!). So the trading of meaningless information NTs do to establish connection feels like walking through cold molasses for the ND person. ND persons tend to want language to literally mean something, not as an invisible social signal they do not tend to get. ND folks also value authenticity, and there is little meaning to them in "fake" conversation. However, if you find something meaningful for them to engage in, *then* you will have an interesting conversation. Given NDs often have narrow ranges of interest (but deep interest within that range), this can be a challenge for the NT person to find avenues of connection to their partner if they do not share their spouse's interests.

> *NT individuals typically connect through small talk; it is a building block to further intimacy. ND individuals connect differently, by connecting through common interests. These conflicting styles of connecting can create some frustration as the building blocks to intimacy are different based on specific brain styles.*

Interrupting

ND: I interrupt a lot because I don't want to forget what I want to tell the other person. Sometimes I also think they have finished talking already and interrupt without realizing it. I don't want to be seen as rude, as I am definitely interested; if anything, interrupting means I am interested in the topic!

NT: They constantly interrupt me! It makes me feel so small and unimportant.

It is never fun to be interrupted or talked over. Within neurodiverse relationships, this is a common problem, and there are a couple of points of origin for this problem. First, the ND individual may have difficulty distinguishing the cadence of a conversation and understanding when the other person is done talking. For example, if the NT spouse pauses to take a breath, it may be interpreted by the ND person that they are done speaking. There may be "blurting" of thoughts as the ND individual fears forgetting their own thoughts, or they want to get out what they were going to say before the topic gets changes. The transitions to new conversations can be hard for the ND person to make the shift, so they hurry to get the information they want to convey "out."

47

However, interrupting is not just an ND problem! It can definitely go both ways. Often the ND partner will apologize if you just say "I want to finish my thought" because they did not even realize that they were interrupting.

> There are many factors that can go into interruptions in communication. ND folks are often aware they will forget what they want to contribute if the conversation goes on too long, they may be unaware of the cadence of conversation, or have difficulty understanding where there is a "pause" that allows for them to insert their ideas. This can lead to what feels like "uneven" communication or frustrations with feeling understood in both partners.

The Outer Space of Feelings

ND: Feelings aren't really describable things for me. It feels like trying to explain what the color green looks like to a blind person in that I genuinely have zero clue how to accurately communicate and convey what I mean. It really makes relationships hard, as I can't communicate love very well at all.

NT: My partner shuts down when overstimulated, and it is like a "still face experiment." I can't read his emotions. He can't pick up on mine. He cannot provide emotional support. It is very lonely and confusing.

There is a stereotype that those who are ND do not have feelings. This is grossly unfair and inaccurate. ND folks do have feelings, and they often feel them *intensely*. They also are capable of intense empathy. However, where this goes awry is the *communication* of the feelings. I have seen ND individuals who intensely love their partners, are committed to them, but have a terrible time communicating that in a way that their partner understands and appreciates. It is very sad to see arrows of love that never land on their target.

What makes matters worse is that the NT partner will confuse this inability to express feelings with their partner as not caring for them. Unfortunately, when we are frustrated we don't always do a good job of expressing our own needs; instead we may complain, criticize, or demand. This is often met with a "deer in the headlights" response, facilitating an emotional shutdown by the ND partner, which the NT person further interprets as not caring. What has been triggered in this process, however, is a very sensitive nervous system for the ND partner (you will learn more about these sensory issues in Chapter 5). The NT partner may be met with a logical argument as to all of the ways the ND partner shows their caring (fight), or they may retreat to their favorite interest (flight), or they may simply not respond at all (freeze). Overload of the nervous system can lead to sensory overload, or a "meltdown." This process often leads to unresolved disputes, stored feelings from previous conflicts, and that can make for an emotional tinderbox. Let's look a bit at why ND partners may have difficulty with feelings in the first place. . .

> *It is a harmful myth that ND individuals do not have feelings; often it is the opposite and they are extremely sensitive to feelings. The difficulty can occur in **expression** of the feelings. This process can get exacerbated in the couple relationship when the ND partner is met with criticism, which can aggravate the difficulty in expressing the very feelings their partner would love to hear.*

Alexithymia

ND: I've always found it really hard to share my feelings with my partner because I just don't know what I am feeling. I normally have to think about my feelings for a long time after they happen before I understand what they were. I feel very deeply, but it just doesn't come out or comes out much later. Sometimes I can tell how my partner is feeling, but other times I am completely in the dark.

NT: One time we were taking a walk and I took a nasty fall, and my partner just looked at me as I lay on the ground bleeding and said, "You'd better get up now." I was dumbfounded that they couldn't even understand that I was hurting as I was literally bleeding!

Alexithymia refers to a difficulty experiencing, identifying, and expressing emotions. Individuals suffering from alexithymia will evidence the inability to recognize emotions and their subtleties and textures (Bermond, et al., 2007). Alexithymia lacks an official diagnosis (that is, it is not in the DSM, a book that classifies mental disorders), but anecdotally has been linked to neurodiversity.

It is akin to having low emotional literacy. Typically, people with alexithymia have difficulty identifying feelings (this is a cognitive function), and they also have difficulty experiencing feelings (this is an emotional function). This naturally leads to difficulties in expressing emotions (a communication function).

There are four biologically based emotions: happy, sad, afraid/surprised, and angry/disgusted. The ND individual can typically express these four emotions, but once the individual moves past these into the nuances of other emotions, they can have a harder time both understanding their emotions as well as expressing them. For some, saying "I'm sorry" is a very large stretch; unfortunately, apologies are repair mechanisms for relationships, and this difficulty can impair couple closeness when the NT partner expects their partner to attempt to make things right when communication has become hurtful to them. Often, the ND partner is internally beating themselves up for not communicating, adding to a wall of shame at being "deficient" in the eyes of themselves and very possibly their partner's eyes.

ND individuals can typically express primary emotions such as happy, sad, afraid/surprised, and angry/disgusted. However, they may have difficulties communicating more subtle feelings. In times of stress or conflict, these difficulties can be exacerbated, leaving the NT partner feeling emotionally abandoned when they most wish to be understood and connected. Expression of their dissatisfaction around this to their partner can inadvertently heighten the distress and unresponsiveness of their ND partner.

Chapter 5:
Neurodiversity and Sensory Issues

ND individuals are susceptible to sensory issues. More commonly they are hypersensitive (overly sensitive), though on some issues ND folks may be hyposensitive (underly sensitive). More NDs tend to be hypersensitive than hyposensitive. This can include the tactile system (touch), the auditory system (sound), the visual system (sight), the gustatory system (taste), or the olfactory system (smell), or some combination thereof. It can also include more subtle systems such as the inner senses such as hunger and elimination, the vestibular system (the sense of movement in relation to gravity), and the proprioceptive system (allows the body to sense its location, movement, and actions) (Lane, Miller, & Hanft, 2000; Wilbarger & Wilbarger, 1991). An individual's response will vary, depending upon the amount and dose of noxious stimuli. Additionally, these types of symptoms are more common in individuals on the autism spectrum than other types of neuro-divergencies. We have yet to utilize NDs superhuman senses in a positive way in our society; it really is an overlooked superpower that could be well utilized in various professions. However, the sensitivities can also cause the ND person distress, which extends into accommodating it in their relational life.

Tactile System (Touch Sensitivity)

ND: We were lying in bed reading, and my wife put her hand on me while holding her Kindle. I just don't care for the sensation. I moved over a bit, but she just moved her hand to follow me. I asked her why she keeps doing it, and she says she just likes touching me, which is sweet, but I finally told her and she got all huffy. I don't know how to handle this situation as I know I hurt her feelings when I don't want to be touched.

NT: For me, I touch him because touching him calms my nerves, and makes me feel safe and loved. It is hard not to feel rejected when he shrugs me off or rolls over.

Touch issues can be perplexing and can manifest in terms of clothing selection, getting substances on one's hands, textures of food, and so on. Sometimes things like sock seams cause aggravation or getting sand on one's skin is unbearable or tags on clothing can feel itchy or rough. Certain food textures may not be tolerated, making variety in food choices limited. For a few, there is hyposensitivity (less sensitivity) around cold temperatures and, much to the concern of loved ones, they will skip a winter coat or wear shorts and flip-flops year round, even in frigid winter temperatures.

Touch issues can extend into a couple's sex life, again in the direction of over-interest in sex due to feeling good, to a complete disinterest in sex due to sensory issues. Spouses who approach the ND person may get rejected, based on the sensory issues. A pattern can occur where one spouse approaches, but after frequent rejection, which is often taken personally, stops approaching their spouse, leaving a stalemate around intimacy, and emotional distance can occur.

> *Sensory issues around touch can affect the couple relationship and get interpreted as relational deficits ("We have an ailing sex life") rather than being understood within the context of sensory distress for the ND partner.*

Auditory System (Noise Sensitivity)

ND: My husband wants to discuss things with me when there is background noise. I have a hard time explaining that the air conditioner, heaters, hum of the refrigerator, competes with their voice. My brain just does not filter this noise out, and so it makes it very hard to understand what he is saying. Then if he gets frustrated that I am not listening, he gets louder, as if that will help!

NT: My wife does not seem to listen. I will start to talk about something, and then she veers off on an unrelated topic. As I get frustrated, my voice tends to raise, and then she wants to leave the room completely. It is so maddening!

ND individuals typically dislike loud noises, and in some cases will put their hands over their ears when something is unbearable.

Some have learned to carry ear plugs so they can have control over their noise environment and avoid discomfort. For some, scraping a chair across the floor can feel painful; for others, ongoing background noise can cause distress.

> *It cannot be stressed enough that auditory sensitivities can impair an ND partner in ways that the NT partner may miss. Most people cope with this by using noise-reducing ear plugs (for example, Loop™ ear plugs) or other ways to decrease this stressor.*

Olfactory System (Smell Sensitivities)

ND: I'm so sensitive to smells that I get a headache and/or I am nauseous from smelling someone's perfume, car fresheners, incense, and cleaning products even when it doesn't seem to bother anyone else.

NT: My partner is highly sensitive to the way things smell, which leaves me doing things like the dishes, cleaning out old containers of food. We've tried different ways to manage this, but if a smell is particularly pervasive they will gag for a few minutes. Cooking can be a nightmare, as if the smell is slightly off, they won't be able to eat the food.

Olfactory sensitivities, while less commonly discussed in the literature, are not uncommon, particularly for those on the autism spectrum. One investigatory study found that greater olfactory sensitivity is correlated with a higher number of autistic traits (Ashwin, et al., 2014). This sensitivity, as noted above, can cause meal times to be challenging. Sometimes meals or activities will need to be aborted due to this sensitivity, and restaurants can be far from enjoyable if one is worried about what scent may cause a gag reflex.

> **ND individuals may have extreme olfactory sensitivities. In certain situations, this can be a blessing (for example, fine wine, anyone?), or it can be a curse (for example, changing diapers).**

Visual System (Visual Sensitivities)

ND: My eyes are extremely sensitive to bright light; sunglasses help a lot. The sensory input leads to overload, and if someone shines a bright light in my eyes I get angry. Flourescent lights are the worst! Having a place at my house that can be pitch black, even while the sun's up, helps.

NT: We've had to put 40-watt bulbs in most of the house, and they still complain that the light is too bright! And they hate the color red; I have had to change clothes-shopping habits and not buy them any red clothes.

ND individuals may also face visual system sensitivities (hyper- and/or hyposensitivities), especially those on the autism spectrum. For example, for those on the autism spectrum, there are differences from NTs in the central nervous systems structures (including the cerebellum, cerebral cortex, limbic system, corpus callosum, basal ganglia, brain stem and neurotransmitters within) (Coulter, 2009). This can then cause symptoms such as poor eye contact, not following where someone else is looking, staring with no apparent purpose, light sensitivity, preference to look at objects rather than people, and much more (Coulter, 2009). Common visual sensitivities include sensitivities to bright light, fluorescent lighting, and even certain colors or patterns such as stripes can be problematic.

> ND individuals may have visual sensitivities that affect daily life. Eye contact is a common social expectation, but may be uncomfortable and limited for an ND partner. Many ND people will say they can concentrate on what someone is saying better if they don't look at the person. However, this behavior often gets interpreted by the NT person as lack of caring, or lack of intimacy, in spite of the fact that not looking at their partner actually helps them connect more efficiently.

Gustatory System (Taste Sensitivities)

ND: My palate is hypersensitive to the point where I gag on all but the blandest of foods. I am a crazy-picky eater.

NT: My partner has gotten much better about trying new foods the longer we have been together. However, when she is stressed, there is a tendency to go back to "old faithfuls." I have gotten used to it, but at the beginning of our relationship it would drive me crazy as I had never eaten so much plain cheese pizza!

ND individuals, especially those on the autism spectrum, are often considered "picky eaters" for most of their lives. Trying new foods can be challenging. This can relate to sensory issues in the gustatory system, and may be combined with sensitivities in textures. As such, food choices may be limited. This can be challenging for an NT partner who wants to eat out, try new things, travel and explore new foods, and so on. ND people often train themselves to try new things but, when under stress, will go back to more "safe" foods. Couple this with a lack of appetite; many times ND folks do not get hunger pangs or do not recognize it until they are in a state of distress. For individuals with ADHD, stimulant medications can also curb appetite. It is not unusual for the partner to have to cajole eating, reminding their ND partner they need to eat or prodding them to take some food so they feel better.

ND individuals are notoriously picky eaters, and earlier in life it is not unusual for them to have stuck to a bland diet of "white foods" such as French fries, chicken nuggets and the like. This is likely due to a combination of gustatory, olfactory, and tactile sensitivities. They may not like how food tastes, smells, and/or feels. Additionally, they may not get alerted to hunger pangs. Often, NT partners are put in the role of coaxing their spouses to eat, or they get frustrated when their partner is left irritable due to simply not eating.

Subtle Systems

ND: I've always been clumsy and poorly coordinated. I walk funny and don't swing my arms, it just never came naturally to me. I drop things right and left. I constantly bump into things, especially doorknobs. You'd think I would be used to them being there!

NT: We no longer eat dinner together. He could not stand the sound of my chewing! I was offended at first, but now I just accept it. But eating separately is not ideal in my book.

Individuals who are ND, particularly those on the autism spectrum, may have difficulties with their vestibular system, proprioception, and interoception. Within the vestibular system, one may see issues with balance that result in more trips or falls. Proprioception is awareness of how one's body is positioned or moving. ND individuals may also lack interoceptive awareness, which means they lack awareness of internal body sensation. Our subtle systems allow an individual to integrate bodily sensations, cognitive processes, and emotions (Craig, 2015), but one or more of these may be muted in ND individuals.

Some suffer "misophonia" whereby a person experiences autonomic arousal (i.e. involuntary fight-or-flight response) to "certain innocuous or repetitive sounds such as chewing, pen clicking, and lip smacking" (Edelstein, Brang, Rouw, & Ramachanan, 2013, p. 296). This causes the ND person to feel anxiety, panic, or rage when exposed to these "trigger sounds."

Lastly, often due to lack of interoceptive awareness, the ND partner will not recognize when they are hungry, thirsty, or fatigued and are at a loss to correct the problem because they seldom recognize there is one. NT partners typically gain the expertise to ask "Have you eaten today?" or "Do you need a break?" as they recognize this challenge to self-care of their spouse/partner.

All of the sensory issues that can be experienced by the ND person can bring challenges into their relationships. This is typically addressed by the ND person learning how important it is to care for their biological operating system, in conjuction with the NT partner reminding them as needed to get hydration, food, and rest.

Impact of Sensory Issues on the Relationship

The sensory issues can impact couple relationships very directly (for example, not wanting to be touched) as well as more indirectly (for example, difficulties going out to restaurants). The ND person expends a lot of energy just getting through the day on planet Earth and managing their sensitivities, often in work or home environments where others do not understand their struggles. Their realities around their own bodies are often disregarded, dismissed, or they are told they are dramatic or making things up. The effect is that the ND person is invalidated, sometimes on a daily basis, which can cause a lifetime pattern of doubting themselves and their own realities. Partners who do not understand these sensory struggles can participate in this process of invalidation, often steeped within their own frustration of not knowing how to navigate the demands of their partner's sensory issues, or even recognizing them as such.

The ND person may feel put upon when their partner asks them to contribute to household chores, child care, etc., because they have expended so much energy throughout the day navigating their own sensory (as well as social) issues. They may even think they have contributed significantly to the relationship, only to have their partner complain that they are not doing their fair share. This is a tricky area for couples, as it is unfair for the NT person to do the majority of daily living tasks that require organizing, scheduling, etc., but the ND person may have expended their energy swimming through a sea of sensory and social issues at school or work.

> *Difficulties in managing sensory issues can cause couple conflict around division of labor in the relationship. The ND person may be expending a great deal of emotional energy to get through their day, which is often a silent struggle not shared with their partner. The NT person gets overloaded with task management and has less sympathy or perhaps understanding of these issues in their partner. This can lead to a slow simmering for both partners; the NT person feels overwhelmed and abandoned by their partner; the ND person feels misunderstood and exhausted by demands being insisted upon by their partner.*

Emotional Dysregulation, Commonly Known as "Meltdowns"

ND: Recently while I was having a meltdown, my wife sat down to talk to me about what I was feeling, and was able to listen to me explain what they are like for me. She has been misinterpreting them as aggression towards her all of our marriage. She was dumbfounded. I can't tell you what a revelation this was for her and our relationship. We were headed towards divorce before this talk. Now that she understands that I cannot change the way I feel during a meltdown and that it doesn't involve hate towards anyone has made a huge difference.

*NT person: When he melts down, he becomes so destructive that it's all I can do to survive. He is no longer physically violent but the emotional damage he does is huge, he'll say everything he can possibly think of to upset me, and then later he won't remember. I understand that, but I still have trouble coping with it. I feel like I'm expected to just weather the storm and get over it, but honestly, he's **so** creatively toxic that it can leave me struggling afterwards for days.*

Meltdowns are not uncommon with ND folks until they gain skills in regulating their internal states in response to either internal or external stimuli. Even then, we all have bad days. Meltdowns are simply an intense reaction to sensory overload. While many NT spouses often see these issues as behavioral problems, the root cause is a neurological problem. This emotional dysregulation can look like tantrums, anger management problems, panic attacks, etc., but what is different is that the origin is due to a vulnerable sensory system. Again, the origin of the problem is not emotional or behavioral; it is sensory. For many ND individuals, there is an over-reactivity to common sensory experiences (Lane, Miller, & Hanft, 2000; Wilbarger & Wilbarger, 1991); it is not uncommon to see an exaggerated startle response when there is a loud noise or unexpected event. Often, ND individuals get mislabeled as having anger-management issues from childhood on, when instead, the issues originate from sensory issues and not primarily from emotional or behavioral issues. Think about having a burr in your pocket that is poking you, but you don't realize it, and no one around you realizes it; you just know there is something that is uncomfortable. This discomfort does not go away but just steadily pokes you as you go about your day. How do you think you might feel and behave?

It is very hard for NTs to understand the level of sensory issues that NDs can face in their daily lives. The ND individual looks perfectly normal, can often perform well at work, but you may come home to someone who is cranky, worn down, or angry. While not every adult who believes they are ND has been diagnosed with a sensory or neurological disorder, even when this is the case, NT partners can become so angry about their needs not being met over time they have a hard time being compassionate to the challenges that may be present in their partner. Both partners get frustrated, and the ND person often lives with a fear that they will never be "good enough" for their spouse and internally lives every day thinking their spouse is on the verge of leaving them. Other ND individuals, either as a defensive posture in response to this threat or due to emotional battering of the spouse who believes their shortcomings are deliberate, will be the ones threatening to end the relationship. Either way, it can lead to attachment anxiety within the relationship where neither spouse can fully relax. They are always waiting for the "other shoe to drop." Good sleep, good nutrition and hydration, and routines can all help to decrease the chances of meltdowns. It can also help to scan the environment for things that cause your specific sensory issues (for example, fluorescent lights, loud or consistent noise, etc.).

Couples can learn the triggers to meltdowns and begin to identify the early warning signs, changing course to avoid meltdowns. The ND partner will often have difficulty, at least initially, noticing these warning signs, so the NT partner may need to give a warning and tell their spouse to take some time to themselves to calm or sooth themselves. The ND individual may find external monitors of fitness (for example, sleep monitoring, pulse rate, etc.) to be helpful indicators that they may be entering meltdown territory (see, for example, www.whoop.com).

> *The first task to prevent meltdowns is to understand what they are and what triggers them for the ND partner. Is it loud noises, social situations, food sensitivities, lack of sleep, or a combination thereof? Doing an analysis of problematic sensory input after meltdowns can lead to how to prevent future problems. Meltdowns are caused neurologically but often are seen as behavioral problems or anger management issues. Couples need to learn how to manage these so that fallout to both partners can be minimized.*

Stimming

ND: I move my thumbs in a geometrical pattern without noticing, or repeat words or phrases. I love that I am now working remotely because I can knit during meetings!

NT: I have noticed my partner does very subtle things when stressed. I catch them tapping their thumb to their other fingers, playing with their hair, tapping their leg. The worst is when they chew their fingernails to the quick. I feel badly for them, but it also does sometimes drive me crazy!

Stimming refers to self-stimulating in some way. It can look very different for different people. Autistic individuals may stim by flapping their hands, rocking, or spinning. But it may take different forms for different people. It may include fidgeting, tapping, humming, whistling, hair twirling, jumping, nail-biting, joint-cracking, teeth-grinding, tongue-clicking, biting the inside of one's mouth, and so on. As a society, we often look down on these types of behaviors, but they help ND individuals manage sensory input. *We all stim* in some way. The purpose of stimming is self-regulation, or calming. It can be in response to sensory issues or strong emotions. Again, due to sensory issues and emotional sensitivity, there is often a greater need for it for ND individuals than NT folks, but we all do these calming behaviors to some extent.

> *Those idiosyncratic little behaviors you have noticed over the years may indeed be "stimming" or ways for an ND partner to self-regulate or calm themselves. NT individuals do it too, but there may be a greater need for the ND partner, based on stressors of living in a neurotypical world, essentially being a stranger in a strange land. It may look like fingernail-biting, hair-twirling, or knee-bouncing but can also be more severe like skin-picking or even head-banging. Stimming is a way to release anxiety or distress from sensory overload.*

Eye Contact

ND: I find it easier to both listen and talk when I am sort of gazing off into the distance or looking blankly at nothing. It helps me to focus on my partner if I do not have to look directly at them. I can handle eye contact for a short amount of time, but it puts a lot of pressure on me. I have to force myself to do it, as I know my partner expects it of me.

NT: It's hard; they never look me in the eye, and seldom say my name. I know they love me, but I really miss that sense of connection. I guess I always believed that the "eyes are the window to the soul" and I've had to revise that notion.

It is not unusual for ND individuals to have difficulties with eye contact. They may have learned to do it over the years, but it is seldom comfortable. Responses can range from slight discomfort at maintaining eye contact, eyes watering, to literally a searing pain. Yet, in our culture around relationships, and especially in romance, we believe "eyes are the window to the soul" and how we connect in the NT world. NT partners often take lack of eye contact as a sign of disconnection or disrespect, when in reality, the ND individual may simply be trying to self-regulate around this sensory issue. I have known more than one ND individual who has been interrogated by police simply because they seemed "shifty" due to lack of eye contact or were not offered a job because they seemed "disinterested."

NTs often interpret the lack of eye contact as disinterest, lack of empathy, or disconnection. If the NT person has low self-esteem, they can interpret the lack of eye contact as confirmation of their own lack of worth. Culturally, we also tend to see eye contact as correlated with trustworthiness. It is important to understand that the ND individual is typically trying to regulate their own anxiety by not looking at you in order for them to be able to connect. At the same time, the ND individual must recognize that their partner connects in this way and make an attempt to look at their partner's face. One trick is to look at your partner's ear as an alternative, or even between their eyebrows, as this can both decrease anxiety and allow your partner to believe you are attempting to connect with them. These suggestions are difficult as it may feel like "masking" and at the same time, you are in a cross-cultural relationship and both partners must make the effort to bridge the space between planets. NTs also should understand that eye contact is a cultural expectation and not necessary for intimacy. Think about a blind person; do you think they are less capable of connecting with their partner? Love does not require eyes. The reality is your partner may be trying hear you by *not* looking at you.

> *In an NT world, eye contact has become a prime commodity indicating interest, intimacy, and connection. For ND individuals, eye contact may cause physical discomfort or indicate too much sensory input as they try to listen. They actually may be trying to listen more closely by not looking at their partner.*

The Impact of Sensory Issues: Showers, Sex, and What's the Deal with Brushing Teeth?

Showers

ND: Baths and showers cause me stress and it feels like an added stress I could do without. Society is obsessed with

people being clean and what they consider presentable.
Yes, we still may need a gentle reminder about hygiene.
Don't say, "You reek," or "Gosh, your teeth are super yel-
low!" Patience is big; try saying "Maybe you should go take
a shower."

NT: I've talked to my boyfriend several times about his hy-
giene. I don't want to mother him, or nag or manipulate
him about it. I adore him, but he doesn't shower enough
and it turns me off. . .

Often hygiene can be a bone of contention in neurodiverse relationships. Some of it is based on societal expectations of how
often we "should" shower or bathe, and some of this is based in
not wanting to be close to someone who has not bathed or show-
ered due to odors, greasy hair, and so on. For the ND person, this
typically comes from sensory issues. The ND partner may not
like the feel or smell of certain soaps or shampoos, or they may
even not like the feel of water on them. It can also relate to not
taking social cues that the lack of hygiene is problematic for others.
I've also seen some people become so ritualized around bathroom
routines (with rituals used to decrease anxiety), that it then becomes an overwhelming task to even get started with showering
or bathing. The difficulty with showering or bathing typically lies
in sensory processing issues (Crane, Goddard & Pring, 2009).

> *What typically lies at the bottom of an ND person's reluctance to bathe or shower is a sensory processing disorder. This makes the task much more challenging than for NT persons and can become a point of contention for couples where the NT partner wants to be close to their partner but finds the hygiene issues off-putting, while the ND partner may lack the energy needed to bathe or shower on a more regular basis.*

Sex

ND: I'm not a touchy-feely person, and when we kiss, I can't wait for it to be over. I enjoy sex when we do have it, but I just never want to have it. He's very sensitive about me not wanting to have sex with him. . . how do I say "It's not you, it's me?"

NT: My boyfriend is on the autism spectrum. We have sex about once a week; the frequency is less than I'd like but the quality is better. The problem is, I am always the one to initiate, and a lot of times I get rejected. He just doesn't have a high sex drive, but I do not know how to not take this personally. I know logically his rejections are not personal, but I still feel really hurt. He knows this, but we get stuck on this. We went on mini vacation, and we had great sex. I asked my boyfriend if he wanted to eat lightly so we could have sex again, and he said "Well, we don't need to worry about that anymore, because we already had sex this weekend!" He sounded so relieved, like it was a chore! I was so upset.

Given that neurodiversity typically affects social interaction, emotions, and bodily and sensory perceptions, sexuality is often affected in some manner for the ND person. However, as in all areas, sexual norms are set by the neurotypical population, causing the ND individual to be pathologized if there are differences from that norm. ND individuals engage in love-based sexuality, but also may engage in pleasure-based sexuality, asexuality, and solitary sex (Bertilsdotter & Jackson-Perry, 2021). It is common for partners to have different sexual appetites; this is often exaggerated in neurodiverse relationships. For autistic individuals, there may be sensory issues that impede sexual connection. For ADHD-affected individuals, they may have a hard time focusing during sex, leaving their partner feeling rejected or inferior if this dynamic is not understood. Anxiety can also impede the desire for sexual connection, and it can also impede sexual performance. For the NT partner, role overload or burnout, coupled with emotional intimacy needs not being met can lead to inhibited sexual desire.

> ND individuals may both have sensory issues related to sexual activity, or anxiety can impede sexual desire. NT partners who suffer burnout often find that their resentment about task overload or emotional intimacy needs not being met dampens sexual desire.

Brushing Teeth

ND: I am sometimes able to get through a full 30 seconds of brushing before I have to stop myself to prevent vomiting. Some days I can only tolerate 15 seconds, and somedays I can't handle brushing my teeth at all, though I always try. My body quivers, twitching, as goosebumps appear on my neck and arms. My brain feels frozen as all of my focus goes into holding back my gag reflex in response to the sensations and strong flavor of toothpaste in my mouth. I don't think many people understand the anguish of brushing your teeth when you have sensory issues (adapted from Anonymously Autistic, 2016).

NT: My wife tries to kiss me, but she never brushes her teeth. I try avoiding her because I can't handle the smell of her breath or the plaque residue on her teeth. I love her, but her lack of hygiene is killing our marriage.

These two examples show the dilemma for couples when sensory issues interfere with teeth brushing. The first example shows the extreme sensitivity that can arise for an ND person and how arduous just brushing one's teeth can be. The second spouse is grossed out by the lack of dental hygiene, and it causes distancing within the relationship.

Are You *Ever* Coming Out of the Bathroom???

*NT: I am so frustrated with the amount of time he spends in the bathroom! Literally **hours** every night. I end up texting him asking him when he is coming out. I'm a toilet widow!*

ND: Why do I spend so much time in the bathroom? It is because I become overloaded with sensory information. The bathroom is devoid of a lot of that. It's usually white with a few accents, quiet, and not a lot of social interaction. I don't usually get bothered when I am in there; no one expects anything of me while I am in the bathroom. It gives me a space to disengage from everything for a while. I like calling the bathroom my "meditation chamber" for that reason. I do this in social situations. I go to the bathroom just for a break. Nobody bothers me there. Once I step foot in the bathroom, I feel an overwhelming sense of peace and safety (assuming it is clean). My muscles are no longer tense, my hands stop jittering, and I am relaxed.

Many people find reprieve in the bathroom, whether it is quiet time, a hot shower, or a luxurious bath. However, for neurodivergent folks, it can be an important coping strategy to spend time away from sensory overload or demanding social situations. This can cause tension when tasks are not getting done, or a spouse feels like they are abandoned, or they feel frustrated that they are left doing household tasks or parenting on their own. For the ND partner, it is not unusual for the intestinal system to be sensitive, with issues such as Irritable Bowel Syndrome impeding functioning. This makes the bathroom a hot-button issue in their relationship, with one spouse feeling like they have been abandoned and the other needing the reprieve of a quiet spot with low sensory activity.

Bathrooms can become a point of contention in neurodiverse relationships. When due to sensory issues (for example, a sensitive digestive tract) or because of the need for sensory reprieve, the bathroom becomes a place of flight for the ND partner. Besides long periods of bathroom entanglement that may inconvenience others, NT spouses can feel abandoned by this behavior, or resentment that tasks go unfinished when their partner takes prolonged flights into the quiescence of the bathroom.

Chapter 6:

Black Holes—Mental Flexibility and "Black-and-White Thinking"

ND: I get an idea in my head of what the future is going to be like, and then it is so hard to change that! I try to take myself less seriously and be less defensive, but it is difficult. My thinking is just stubborn.

NT: It has been helpful to know there are some things my wife just doesn't naturally understand. My wife says that being my partner has helped her grow and experience new things, and for me it's helped bring structure, routine, and stability to my life.

Neurodiverse individuals often have difficulty with mental flexibility. This, in part, is due to living in a strange land with limited abilities to interpret social cues and how they should behave. This typically leads to the following features:

- An insistence on sameness with regard to daily rituals or routines
- Inflexibility to changes to these rituals and routines

- Difficulty navigating changes as they occur in a daily environment.

Typically, these features are caused by the need to manage anxiety. Sameness, rituals, and routines can provide predictability, which is soothing for the ND person.

There are different types of flexibility, and ND individuals may have difficulties with one or more of the types of flexibility needed to adapt to change. Borrowing from the field of leadership, there are three types of flexibility; ND individuals may have difficulties in one or more of these areas.

> *In order to manage sensory issues and/or anxiety, ND individuals will often resort to sameness in daily rituals and routines. Difficulty can occur, however, when rituals or routines need to be changed due to obligations around children, vacations, or other everyday crises that may occur.*

Cognitive Flexibility

ND: I feel like my brain is constantly scanning and processing analytically to try and be as efficient as possible in almost everything I do in everyday life. I'm constantly taking in various factors and analyzing and evaluating cause and effect; "If I do x it leads to y", "It would be better to know the result of y before I get around to x, so I should chase up y first", "It makes sense to do these tasks in this order because. . ." I almost always come up with the right answer, which she admits that I am usually right. In the midst of this process, my wife often interrupts, and it throws off my thinking and I admit I get mad.

NT: He was going on a trip, and I wanted to do something nice so I asked if I could make him a ham sandwich. But then I realized we were out of ham, and I was afraid to offer an alternative due to fear of his explosions. I just don't know when he is going to take things badly. I feel like I walk on eggshells all of the time.

There is cognitive flexibility that requires using different thinking strategies to manage the situation at hand. Cognitive flexibility allows an individual to hold multiple scenarios in their mind and see when a shift is needed (Center for Creative Leadership, 2021). Lack of cognitive flexibility leads to what has been commonly termed "black-and-white thinking" or "binary thinking." Things are either "right" or "wrong." This may do well for the ND people in their career where they are rewarded for being "right," but when they shift into their personal relationships, it can cause conflict. In this couple's case, this intensive thought process has led his wife to be fearful of interrupting him, thus causing some resentment and distance in the relationship. The ND spouse's lack of cognitive flexibility caused a cycle of explosions, which caused her to retreat and be tentative in everything she communicated to him. Black-and-white thinking is typically due to anxiety or emotional arousal and can lead to impulsive decisions. It can lead to seeing one's partner as "all bad" or "all good" in times of distress. Blaming is not uncommon when this occurs. This thinking style can be adjusted as a person learns to think in shades of gray; cognitive behavioral therapy can be helpful when this issue impinges upon an individual or relationship.

Emotional Flexibility

ND: My partner accuses me of not supporting them. I get defensive and tell them all of the ways I have been sup-

porting them. I don't know how many times I can explain to them, with specific examples, of how I support them. This doesn't seem to matter, it falls on deaf ears. It is so frustrating.

NT: I really try not to get into an argument because they last forever, and she keeps telling me I am wrong to feel the way I do. I always think she is much smarter than me, and that I should listen, but honestly, I am worn out. She never really hears how I am feeling, and instead I feel like I am presenting my case and she is a lawyer dissecting my logic.

There is emotional flexibility that requires focus on the other person in order for you to understand their emotions and change how you approach that person so that you can connect with them. This means the ND person may have difficulty in changing their reaction in response to your reaction. Emotional flexibility requires hearing the other person's grievances and not shutting down. Inflexibility is evidenced by a dismissing of concerns and emotions of the other person (Center for Creative Leadership, 2021). In our example above, the ND individual is caught in defending the logic of them not being supportive. They have a hard time understanding their partner does not care about their "evidence" of support but cannot shift into their NT partner's emotional world of feeling unsupported and find out what their partner needs to feel supported. Instead they get caught in an endless loop of defending themselves, only to lead to both partners feeling frustrated and disconnected.

> *This is a common difficulty in neurodiverse relationships. Often, NT partners are looking for emotional validation with a strong need to feel understood; ND partners have a hard time making this shift according to their partner's needs and will stay in the vein of a logical argument, attempting to solve the problem at hand. It represents two different views of conflict—the NT partner wants to have their feelings heard; the ND partner wants to have their logic validated and the problem solved.*

Dispositional Flexibility

ND: I am constantly labeled a pessimist, but I prefer the term "realist." I find constantly having jolly people around me really annoying. My pessimism is me and no amount of negative criticism from optimistic people will stop it or cure it!

NT: I don't really think my partner is a pessimist, but they can seem quite negative. What I can say from personal experience is that people assume she is a pessimist because of the way she talks about things, even though she is a pretty happy and content individual.

Dispositional flexibility is what allows an individual to see a situation realistically but remain optimistic in the face of whatever event is occurring. They will acknowledge difficulties but be able to visualize how things can change and be better, and they can tolerate this ambiguity (Center for Creative Leadership, 2021).

There are a lot of things for an ND person that can get in the way of dispositional flexibility including anxiety, past negative or traumatic experiences, or just intolerance of abnormally cheerful people, which they are likely to interpret as inauthentic. However, as in our example above, the ND partner is actually pretty content but gets misread by others. Indeed, the ND individual's reliance on problem solving may enable them to be less passionate about things that bother NTs and remain more flexible when evaluating situations with heightened emotionality than their NT counterparts.

> ND partners often have an advantage of being able to evaluate emotional situations more dispassionately than their NT counterparts. They are often realists, which can come off as pessimism to others when they don't actually feel negative or pessimistic.

Emphasis on Fairness and Justice

ND: I always find that I am complaining in my head about some imbalance in my relationship. It could be about chores, love, sex, whatever, but it is always about my perceived lack of fairness. If I do something for my partner, I find I expect something in return, a "quid pro quo" of sorts. I feel like, in my relationship, there is an unspoken expectation of equivalent exchange. Sometimes it feels more like a competition, rather than based on love.

NT: I get so tired of having to do the majority of scheduling and organizing, and then when I hear "that's not fair" from my wife, it just sends me. She has a whole system in her head of what she thinks is "fair," and has a hard time understanding all that I put into the relationship. We end up arguing about stupid things like who last cleaned the toilet, or who last unloaded the dishwasher. It is exhausting.

ND folks are often quite honest and will fight for fairness and justice in their lives and for others. Expect that if something does not feel fair or just for ND individuals, you will likely have a reaction from them in a quest for justice. This can sometimes be fatiguing for the NT spouse, yet there is a pureness about the ND person when they fight for the rights of others, or they care for the ethical treatment of animals and the environment, or they want to right power imbalances in society, and so on. However, within relationships, it can lead to an unhealthy score keeping of things that are not really measurable. Additionally, the ND spouse will sometimes get stuck on something they consider unfair and perseverate on it. Perseveration is when a person has an involuntary thought or behavior that continues in spite of a desire for it to stop. Thus, old topics that couples thought were laid to rest will sometimes reappear much to the chagrin of the NT partner who thought it had been a topic addressed and retired.

One of the most endearing things about neurodivergent individuals is their emphasis on justice and fairness, with strong values in these areas. However, in neurodiverse relationships, these qualities can lead to prolongued discussions of things they believe to be unfair or unjust.

Transitions

ND: I hate changes in routine so much! Even if it is some-thing I know I will eventually enjoy, like a vacation, it causes me anxiety. **Tell** *me if my routine is going to be in-terrupted! Sudden changes to routine will lead to over-stimulation.* *I* **need** *routine or I will go bonkers. Transitions are always a challenge to my equilibrium.*

NT: My wife has very specific ideas of how things should be done. If we vary from that, she goes bonkers. I try to remain flexible myself, but the rigidity if something just comes up is maddening. We have little kids, and life just does not go as expected!

Changing gears for ND persons can be particularly challenging for them and for their partners! One way that ND partners cope with anxiety is to keep strong rituals and routines. This goes well until it doesn't, as in the example above when the partner describes the flexibility needed in coping with small children.

Additionally, as previously noted, there is evidence that ND individuals tend to engage in hyperfocus, which causes difficulties diverting attention between tasks (Ashinoff & Abu-Akel, 2019; Ward, Wender, & Reimherr, 1993). This makes transitions and interruptions more difficult, and often the NT partner feels ignored as their spouse is completely engrossed in whatever they may be doing. Video games are a common way for an ND person to de-stress and rejuvenate, but they can create a path to outer space where the NT person believes they have lost their partner; meanwhile household chores, child care, etc., piles up on their lap. The ND person is caught between taking time to recalibrate so they can be a better partner and being present so they can assist their partner. This dance seldom goes well until both individuals understand what is needed and how these breaks can support their connection to each other.

Additionally, the rigidity in thinking often accompanies neurodivergence, again centering more around those on the autism spectrum. The belief that things should be done in a certain way, in a certain order, at a certain time can be difficult to challenge. Psychotropic medications can sometimes help loosen the rigid thinking by decreasing anxiety, which can give both partners some relief.

> **Both due to reliance on rituals and routines and due to hyperfocus on topics at hand, ND individuals may show resistance to change and transitions. This can be frustrating for NT spouses, especially those who enjoy more spontaneity.**

Perseveration

*ND: I have the habit of repeating myself sometimes in an annoying loop that it really annoys my partner. I am trying to stop, but it is so hard. . . something about it is soothing to me. I also feel like I remember every bad thing I've done on a weekly/monthly basis. Not **everything**, of course, but there's probably 100–300 rotating memories.*

NT: When we have an argument, I find my partner goes back over it, over and over again. He just won't drop it. He brings up the same points over and over, and it just feels like he is never going to let it drop.

So you know those passionate interests that your ND partner has? That also can be a function of neurology. That's the upside of their beautiful brain. The downside can be what is termed "perseveration." This is when the ND person has difficulty in shifting from a thought or frame of mind, or even from an activity or task.

This is particularly hard in relationships when the ND person has a great memory and can't let go of an argument. Indeed, while the NT individual may still be steeped in the emotional unfairness of an argument, the ND person may perseverate on the logical basis of the argument. This can cause a constant rehashing of perceived slights or full-blown fights. The ND partner wants their logic understood the NT spouse wants their feelings understood, and the dance continues. This is not an unusual pattern in many relationships, but can be exaggerated with neurodiverse traits.

It can also manifest in repetition of speech, where the ND person repeats themselves over and over, even though their partner has acknowledged what they are saying. It is not typically done on purpose to aggravate others, but the brain seems to get "stuck" in this mode.

Lastly, it can also manifest as obsessive compulsive disorder (OCD) symptoms, such as thinking the same thought over and over again, stuck in a loop that is hard to get out of. Obsessions, however, are generally more severe and accompanied by rituals to reduce the stress of the thought or behavior. Neurodivergent individuals may also suffer Obsessive Compulsive Disorder (OCD), but sometimes the stuckness on a particular thought or behavior is due to perseveration, not full-blown OCD.

> *Perseveration is when an ND partner gets "stuck" on a topic, behavior, or line of thought and can't vary from it. This can lead the ND person to repeat themselves or rehash old arguments. NT partners often try to avoid this by avoiding, feigning interest, getting angry, or saying things to get their partner off the topic.*

Masking and the "But When We First Met. . ."

ND: For years I tried to be "normal." I would watch people interact, and I learned to make "scripts" for myself to communicate with other people. Masking uses up 100% of my brain CPU just trying to analyze all of the interactions going on around me, and respond appropriately.

NT: My wife was really attentive when we first met, but after we married she went back to her video games, and it is really hard to get her attention. I feel rather tricked; she was like a different person before we got married. She was really attentive and focused on me.

Most ND people feel they are from a different planet, but in order to thrive on this one they must learn to fit in. This creates what is called "masking," which is just as it sounds; you put on a different face in order to fit in. It is not the same as being dishonest; it is about surviving in a neurotypical world that devalues your brain style, approach to life, and life experiences. The ND person learns to mimic what they hear others say and that there are certain "scripts" that are called for in certain situations. Again, imagine being dropped off on another planet with a different species. What would you do to fit in to ensure your survival? You would

85

observe, mimic, and learn the language and mannerisms. That is masking. The problem is that the person never feels truly authentic, and it is exhausting and compromises mental health. One study has found that masking or "camouflaging" one's autism in order to fit into social situations combined with unmet support needs increased risk of suicidality (Cassidy, Bradley, Shaw, Baron-Cohen, 2018). At the very least, ND individuals can suffer anxiety, depression, stress, and fatigue.

I often hear spouses complain that their partner does not "*seem* autistic" or "isn't that bad" and because of their own exhaustion have little empathy for the disabling aspects of the neurodiversity. It is extremely common to hear "well, they were able to do _____ when we first met." Or they state that their partner put in great effort at the beginning of the relationship, but then the affection they came to rely on drastically decreased after awhile. This is typically an effect of masking, which we all do. No relationship stays shiny and new, and we don't perform the same behaviors years later as we did when courting. However, for an ND individual, they did put effort in and then once they became comfortable, reverted to putting their efforts into daily survival (for example, getting through the work day, social anxiety, managing their sensory issues, etc.). This leaves the NT spouse feeling cheated and they may accuse their partner of withholding affection or attention. Sometimes this perception of being cheated can fester into a simmering rage that seeps into everyday interactions for the couple.

Conversely, the ND partner feels barraged with demands that they feel they can never adequately meet, and it puts them in fight, flight, or fright mode (with their sensory issues, this state is seldom far away), and then they end up being less able to be responsive to their partner. Thus, a frustrating dance of criticism and defensiveness often launches. The NT person has an internal dialogue of "Why don't they care for me?!" and the ND person has a dialogue (sometimes spoken but often unspoken) of something like "What did I do now?"

> *The reality is that we all "mask" when we are in a new relationship. However, as time wears on, we let these masks drop and become more ourselves. For ND partners, this is actually a statement of comfort about their NT partner when they believe they can drop the mask and be themselves. However, the NT partner often longs for some of the acts or verbal confirmations of love that occurred early in the relationship and feels tricked when these behaviors drop off as comfort in the relationship increases.*

DIFFERENT PLANETS. . .

Chapter 7:
The Time-Space Continuum:
Executive Functioning Issues

ND: Every time I have a huge bout of anxiety and I can't do executive functions, it makes me feel more out of control and panicked and trapped in the behaviors that ruin my life. Like sitting zoned out on the couch. Sometimes my meds are less effective and old habits are getting harder to overcome every day, and it makes me feel pretty hopeless.

NT: Getting out the door is a major challenge at our house, and I must continually remind my partner of appointments, chores, and even hygiene. And the indecision that can happen makes me crazy. Just a question like "What do you want for dinner?" can cause them to shut down or worse, throw a fit.

For some, communicating with an ND individual can feel like they are in another time-space continuum. This ranges from complaints that the ND person constantly "spaces out" to daily living tasks such as chores, child care, and appointments. This is typically due to challenges with what is termed "executive functioning." Executive functioning is about getting things done; it includes organizing, planning and scheduling, and prioritizing. It also includes listening to instructions and encoding things into memory. Many ND individuals have executive functioning limitations. In this chapter, we will explore this issue of paying attention and executive functioning challenges including time blindness, planning, scheduling and organizing, as well as memory issues and their impact on generalized learning. Lastly, when executive functioning systems are not working well, we may see ND individuals responding in impulsive ways, leaving others wondering who the alien is in their living room.

> *Executive function relates to the "doing" part of our brain, and typically this is a challenging area for ND persons. It can result in feelings of paralysis, frustration, anger, or even meltdowns. Procrastination can be a steady companion for those with executive functioning difficulties, and NT partners will see "random" selection of tasks by the ND individual when impulsiveness takes over in response to some panic.*

Paying Attention: Earth to. . .

ND: I find myself spacing out on what feels like a repetitive conversation even if the details are new. It's a reminder to do a chore, remembering a detail my partner mentions, etc. It really frustrates my wife.

NT: He always fidgets, never hears when I start speaking and I can say like three sentences before he turns to me and asks me to repeat everything I just said. It is exhausting.

For many ND individuals, paying attention within daily conversations is a major chore. This may mean that they zone out during conversations, leaving their partner feeling ignored or devalued. Additionally, a common coping strategy for the ND person may include mindlessly agreeing, only to backtrack later and say "I never agreed to that!" There are many potential reasons for attention problems. For those with ADHD, it is obvious; inattentiveness is part of their diagnosis. But those on the autism spectrum often have auditory processing issues that impair their ability to interpret what they hear (Ocak, et al., 2018). Attention problems can also be linked to social anxiety, PTSD, and depression. Partners who do not understand this dynamic can get exasperated trying to talk to their loved one and must learn adaptations to get their partner to hear everyday conversation. Others cope by finding "tricks" to get their partner's attention, being sure to say their name prior to speaking, or check to see that they are listening to ease frustration with this problem.

> *It is not uncommon for an ND partner to experience auditory processing issues and have difficulties with attention and/or memory of conversations. This can cause the NT partner frustrations, especially when they internalize this as their partner not caring for them because they have difficulties hearing what has been said.*

Time Blindness

ND: An hour can feel like three minutes and vice versa. I end up being late and have a hard time sticking to any schedule. It's embarrassing.

91

> *NT: He has a hard time with time management. I find myself wanting to snap at him when it's time to leave and he's still finding his keys, finishing up a game, etc.*

NT folks typically have a sense of the passage of time and can guess how long things will take, how much time has passed, and so on. Individuals with executive-functioning issues genuinely struggle to estimate how long a task will take. As such, school and work assignments can suffer, and spouses get frustrated with continued lateness, procrastination, or missed appointments. There are many reasons for these foibles that fall under this executive functioning, including:

- Relying on faulty short-term memory instead of writing things down;
- Taking on too many commitments, due to difficulties estimating how much time the commitments will take;
- Difficulties calculating travel time;
- Difficulties with transitions (for example, leaving one meeting to go to another, or shifting family activities);
- Losing watches, phones with electronic calendars, planners, etc., that keep the ND partner on track (Harris, n.d.).

As the ND partner struggles to live in a time-bound neurotypical world, they develop coping strategies. They may be very time-centric, becoming focused down to the minute or second, or they may be completely unaware of time and see little need to go by the clock. Both coping styles can be frustrating for the partner, who either must keep to the strict schedule established by the ND partner, or they are corralling, trying to get their partner to abide by normal time constraints life imposes.

Additionally, stories in life are about time; they have a beginning, middle and an end. Yet the ND partner may have a hard time organizing stories due to difficulties with time. When asked what happened during their day, they may have a hard time responding or be unable to put the story into words. Partners may grill them with the who, what, where, when, why, and how, only to find their partner unable to construct the story in a meaningful way. Again, without knowledge of this dynamic, the NT partner may believe the ND spouse is not willing to share or even hiding things, when sharing is not easy for their husband/wife/partner.

> *"Time blindness" is a common executive functioning issue for ND partners, much to the chagrin of their NT partners. This may mean the NT person has to be the one to "keep the clock" and ensure events occur, items are found. The NT person deals with procrastination, and the inevitable panic procrastination brings, on a regular basis.*

Planning, Scheduling, and Organizing

ND: Planning is one of my biggest issues. While I managed to get a promotion at work, I had to step down because I couldn't organize everything I needed to do. I just can't plan things worth a darn, and have trouble breaking tasks into smaller tasks. I also have no innate sense of where things should go when I am not using them, and things end up sprawled all over the place anyway. It is hard not to feel like I am letting people down all the time.

NT: I'm super organized, and I know I just can "do" things for my partner, but sometimes I don't know how to help. I do reminders a lot, but neither of us want me watching over him; I'm not his mom. I have empathy for his situation, but I must admit I can't relate. I offer direct help when I can. I take a lot of organizational tasks upon my-

*self, though I can't, and don't want to, assume all of them.
I discourage his negative self-talk as much as I can.*

Another challenge common to those with neurodiversity is problems with the executive functioning skills of planning, scheduling, and organizing. As with our couple above, there is not a surety of how to work as a team. The ND partner needs some support, but the NT partner is clear she does not want to fall into the role of mother, and both partners need to feel independence and competence. She is unclear how to help, and this is a common dilemma to navigate for neurodiverse couples. The person with the executive functioning skills is hesitant to "take over" yet sees tasks that need to get done, many of which need to occur in a timely way. How do couples balance this effectively?

This can lead to the NT spouse shouldering a disproportionate amount of family duties, potentially leading to burnout from excessive labor (emotional and physical labor). This can also lead to issues such as procrastination, for example, or impulsivity when the ND person decides "randomly" to pick something to do off their "list" that does not really make sense in the current time. The ND partner can feel like they are being constantly nagged, criticized and/or micromanaged. Given that things need to get done and if your NT partner has superior executive functioning skills, it can lead the ND individual feeling "less than" or like a failure. Sometimes the ND partner develops a habit of saying what their partner wants to hear just to get them off their back, only to have backlash when tasks do not get completed or appointments get missed. This coping style inevitably does not work in the long run and creates more friction.

> *It is a developmental task of a neurodiverse couple to figure out how to balance executive functioning issues of planning, scheduling, and organizing. There needs to be a team approach that does not overly tax either partner, but ultimately the NT partner often shoulders the executive functioning. ND partners can lessen this burden by learning organizational skills, using calendars, electronic reminders, and so on. NT partners need to communicate their limits to their ND partners, and efforts need to be made to make this difference as equitable as possible.*

Memory and Generalized Learning Issues

ND: I was diagnosed with autism-spectrum disorder and ADHD, and my memory in general is horrible. I can't remember much until the right keywords/phrases are said, and then it's like a swell of information, like watching or experiencing a short movie. Then I do remember. But until that occurs, I don't remember much. My brain is a permanent repository of useless facts, though.

NT: Well, I am trying to learn how to live with this trait in my partner. She can't remember why she walked into a room. If I don't make a shopping list, even if it is just for three items, she will only come home with one. It is super frustrating though, because it seems, in some areas, her memory is far superior to mine!

95

Due to executive-functioning problems, ND individuals can find some tasks particularly arduous, especially if those tasks are not intrinsically interesting. There is a cacophony of outside stimuli that is distracting, as well as internal thoughts around failure. It can be hard to make it to the starting line. There is a decrease in motivation and problems with task initiation, in what looks like procrastination, until there is a fast-approaching deadline OR perhaps an angry partner (I've heard this described as "nature's Ritalin," which is fitting!).

There is evidence that neurodivergent individuals have difficulty with working memory, which refers to the brain's ability to hold information, work with it, and connect the information to other information (Rabiee, et al., 2020). What happens for some neurodivergent folks is that they may not remember all the steps of what they are doing, or they might not remember the information in the correct order. The information then must also get put away for long-term storage; this does not always occur, or it may occur in a more haphazard way. What I hear from NT clients is that they can't understand why they have to keep going over and over things. They don't understand why their ND partner can remember some things, but not others (like their birthday or anniversary, for example). Anxiety, depression, and/or trauma can heighten this condition. Additionally, sensory issues may cause the ND person to have a lot of "static" that can get in the way of concentrating on what is being said.

All of these issues can lead the ND partner to feel overwhelmed and pretty consistently run negative thoughts through their minds about what failures they are. Likewise, this puts the NT partner in charge of many things that need to be done, and this can create a swirl of resentment that feeds back into the ND partner's feeling of failure. The failure may be disguised as anger or withdrawal, but underneath, there is often a feeling of horror that they again let their partner down. Most people have a hard time accomplishing tasks in this mind-state, and a cycle gets put in motion. At times the feelings of failure are too much, and a defense against it is to blame the partner or escape in some way, such as into their special interest, or less helpfully, substances or other negative coping behaviors.

> *It is extremely frustrating for both partners when there are memory problems evident. NT partners typically get frustrated when they explain things about themselves, especially about their inner desires or needs, and this does not get remembered by the ND partner. This can bring feelings of failure for the ND partner, the flames of which get fanned by an angry NT partner who does not feel cared for.*

Impulsiveness

ND: ADHD causes you to regulate stimuli differently. That's why our emotions are so big in one moment, and gone the next. It is hard to regulate how you feel and behave.

NT: My partner always has to call out, loudly, anything they see as an offense or injustice. She admits that it might not help the situation, but it makes her feel better in the moment. She doesn't mind if she comes off as rude, as in her mind, she is in the right. Sometimes, it is just embarrassing.

Impulse control can be an issue both for individuals on the spectrum and those with ADHD. In our examples here, there are different reasons for impulsiveness. The first is the difficulty with emotional regulation and how big feelings can feel. In the second, when their ND partner goes on a rampage, it is triggered by moral outrage. ND folks tend to have strong feelings about morality (which is a good thing!), but then have difficulty when the world does not confirm to their beliefs. They can get entrenched in the moral dimension, argue it, and believe they are right, failing to take into account the other person's thoughts or feelings.

The impulsiveness may also be due to impaired executive functioning. If it seems like a person is doing something "out of the blue" it may be because that thing has long been held on a list, seemingly random or unimportant, but with their difficulties with organizing and prioritizing, just gets "pulled" from the list of things that they have been meaning to do for sometime. This impaired executive functioning may also cause impulsiveness or difficulties with "stream of consciousness" speech (for example, monologuing). It may also show up as interrupting others when they are talking so that they don't lose their train of thought (or they don't understand the social cues that the other person was not yet done with their end of a conversation).

> *Impulsive and chaotic behaviors can strain relationships. Impulsivity for an ND person may be caused by overstimulation, emotional dysregulation, or executive functioning problems. NT partners in the line of fire may find themselves blamed, or caught in an argument with no good end in sight.*

Chapter 8:
Living in a Strange World—
Anxiety and Depression and their
Sequela

*ND: I have these crazy moments when I feel there might be rejection coming on, and I freak out, and seem to get depressed and negative. There seems to be this vicious cycle where I get anxious and depressed about the relationship ending, and of course my partner gets weary of my anxiety and depression, only making me **more** worried that they will leave.*

NT: I don't understand. He does not appear to be motivated to want to be close to me! He never tries and always forgets what is important to me.

If you were picked up and dropped on another planet where you could not understand the rules of conduct or how you should communicate with the species living there, how would you feel? One of the most common symptoms for those who are neurodiverse is anxiety or depression, and they are often coupled or "comorbid." It is well documented that those on the autism spectrum suffer anxiety and depression, with roughly half suffering a mood disorder (cf. Hofvander, et al., 2009; Lungnegård, et al., 2011; Gaman, et al., 2017). The same is true for those with ADHD (CHADD, 2019). Further, depression and anxiety interfere with thinking, concentration and memory (Christopher & McDonald, 2005), which takes us back to impaired executive functioning.

Generalized Anxiety

The most common byproduct of neurodiversity is anxiety. Indeed, research has begun to see this link. For example, an exploratory study of adults with autism diagnoses found that childhood sensory-processing issues follows into adulthood with consequent emotional dysregulation and, for adults, an anxiety disorder diagnosis (McMahon, et al., 2019). The absolute paralysis that occurs is a common point of contention in couples. NT partners may have told their partner what they need for years, only to have it seemingly ignored. This gets personalized, of course, and what is missing is the understanding of the absolute sheer level of anxiety that the ND person must traverse in order to take action in life. There is correlational evidence that children on the autism spectrum who are hyper-responsive around sensory issues also suffer anxiety (Schauder & Bennetto, 2016); this patterned response often appears to get internalized in adulthood. This also makes sense historically for many ND individuals in that their differences often lead to negative messages they have received in childhood, about who they are. As ND children, messages by family or school often include pejoratives such as "difficult," "challenging," "noncompliant," "spoiled," "dramatic," and so on. These messages get carried into adulthood and become, metaphorically, a very tall mountain to climb just to engage in an everyday task.

Social Anxiety

ND: I've been struggling with anxiety and insecurity over every last detail of my life. I feel like an imposter 24/7. I can write just fine, but if I have to have a verbal conver-

100

sation with someone I don't know, my anxiety spikes and I don't speak clearly. I much prefer email! I just don't think I explain things clearly, and even my partner gets confused by what I say. While emails are stressful, phone calls and talking in person are significantly worse. I suffered a lot of bullying when I was younger, and I have a social hypervigilance. When I am having strong feelings, it is hard to stay present, and it is all too easy to fall into unhealthy routines.

NT: My boyfriend is on the spectrum and has mad social anxiety, which manifests even if he's around people he knows. His coping mechanism is to hide from social gatherings for hours on his phone or he tries not to go at all. It creates a very awkward situation, where I don't really know what to tell people. It's at a point where it feels disrespectful towards my family and I feel embarrassed to have to say he is locked in a room, like our relationship is in turmoil, when it is not.

Again, with neurodiversity often affecting social interaction, anxiety around relationships and being in social situations is common. Often, this is related to over- or understimulation and sensory issues (as opposed to social anxiety disorder in neurotypicals). Social anxiety is a common clinical concern for those on the autism spectrum (White, et al., 2012), and about 30% of those with ADHD suffer social anxiety (Kessler, et al., 2006). If both partners are more introverted, this is less of an issue, but if one wishes more social contact, they may see their partner as deficient. Others work out systems where they acknowledge and respect these differences, and cope by doing things like taking two cars to social events, so the ND partner can depart when they feel overloaded by either the social contact and/or sensory issues (for example, loud conversation, music, etc.).

Task Paralysis

ND: I broke down crying yesterday because I realized an hour had passed since I meant to leave to go to the store. I'm really jealous of people who can just go do things. It's so unfair that every time I try to do something simple, I end up distracted and trying to do six other things. This happens over and over again and I chastise myself for it; I just feel so powerless.

NT: I asked him to vacuum, and he said "Okay, in a minute." He then proceeded to have a breakdown about not being a good enough husband as he wasn't able to vacuum in the minute as promised. It's awful to see him be so hard on himself, and it is frustrating for me that small tasks seem so big to him.

When each day is filled with anxiety, some days are better than others, often depending upon how an individual is fulfilling their self-care needs. ND individuals can be quite talented, yet can struggle to get things done (often due to executive-functioning challenges). Their abilities and accomplishments may not be congruent, leaving their partners struggling to understand how they can be so talented in some areas of their life but struggle to complete simple things such as making a phone call, getting the laundry done, or emptying the dishwasher. The uneven performance at best perplexes the partner, at worst infuriates them when they are left doing more of the mundane tasks in the home. The ND partner often is not a good judge of their abilities and energy, and will make promises to do something, but when they hit a wall of anxiety, fail to deliver, much to the dismay of their partner.

Repetitive Behavior

ND: I have a daily routine, and if that gets messed up, I get nervous or angry, and it can sometimes lead to a meltdown. When I get up, I have my routine to get ready for work down to a science. I wake up 30 minutes before having to be at work: I have a three-minute shower, a four-minute dry-off/hygienic prep, and a quick breakfast. I get really frustrated when I have to deviate from this plan!

NT: My girlfriend has some weird quirks, which I know are from her autism. She has to start the day and end the day in exactly the same order. If I interrupt her, she gets upset.

One way that some ND people deal with anxiety is through repetitive behavior or thoughts. This can take a variety of forms, including tapping of feet or hands, keeping the order of activities or items the same, or repeating a phrase, word, or story. It can even take the form of just watching the same TV show over and over again. Repetitive behavior can help decrease the arousal of the nervous system (meaning it decreases anxiety), which is why we see it in neurodiversity. When repetitive behaviors are compulsions to deal with obsessions, the individual may be diagnosed with Obsessive Compulsive Disorder (OCD). OCD is a form of neurodiversity, and again we may see overlap with other neurodiverse brain styles (Autism Spectrum or ADHD).

Additionally, there is a tendency for ND brains to "need" pattern completion. For example, one man kisses his wife in a pattern of three. It can look like superstition, but at the crux of the behavior is an internal need to complete a pattern.

> *Repetitive behavior is calming for those who are ND. This need for ritual and routine can sometimes get taken to an extreme, however, with behaviors that can look like OCD symptomology. There is also a strong need for pattern completion, thus we may see behaviors repeated as a way to meet this need.*

The Trauma of Living in an NT World/PTSD

ND: I was heavily bullied for my special interest in childhood. I find it hard to talk to people because I fear being mocked, even with perfectly nice people. I also get paranoid about boring or annoying people. As an adult, I find it unbearably hard to ask others for help or clarification, including my partner. I had many experiences growing up that resulted in me crying because I couldn't understand a concept, handle criticism, or speak up for myself. I'm just worried others are going to dislike me for anything I say or do. Due to my traumatic experiences with bullying as a child, I learned to ignore the faintest of feelings and had to adapt this numb mask I carried everywhere. I still felt a lot, but couldn't express it or talk about it. It eventually developed into major depressive and anxiety disorders, where I couldn't handle living with so much muddy feelings I was holding back.

NT: My partner constantly monologues. Over the years I began to understand that they have developed this habit due to a history of being misunderstood. They have this need to overexplain everything. They worry they are going to get the words wrong. It can be exhausting, but I get that they were invalidated and gaslighted a lot growing up.

It is not unusual for an ND individual to have been significantly emotionally (and sometimes physically) battered by living in an NT world. They may have been bullied in school, misunderstood, negatively labeled, or cast aside in some way. If they haven't learned adequate self-advocacy skills, this bullying or maligning may continue into adulthood. ND individuals often build emotional walls around themselves for protection and will even go so far as to limit relationships or discount their importance. The ND person may vacillate between flight, fright, or freeze responses that can severely impact the relationship. There is a constant hypervigilance or scanning the environment for signs of danger, which includes relational danger. Add to this repeated daily exposure to conditions that are aversive to the person's nervous system, and it is a lot to navigate for both the individual and the couple.

Symptoms of PTSD that may manifest include unwanted, upsetting memories, nightmares, flashbacks, emotional distress upon exposure to reminders of the trauma, or physical reactivity upon exposure to reminders of the trauma. The individual will often avoid trauma-related stimuli that remind them of thoughts, feelings, or other reminders of the original trauma. It may also cause the person to have increased irritability or aggression, hypervigilance, or heightened startle reaction, among other symptoms (American Psychiatric Association, 2013). There is elevated risk of PTSD both for those on the autism spectrum (Rumball, 2019), as well as those with ADHD (Spencer, et al., 2016). This likely occurs in part due to an elevated fear circuitry in ND individuals.

Living in an NT world, in and of itself, can bring trauma to the ND person. For example, they regularly experience sensory invalidation. It is extraordinarily common for an ND individual to complain about something sensory ("it is too hot," "too

105

crowded," "too noisy," etc.), only to be told that perception is inaccurate or ridiculous. Communication differences for those who are ND are labeled as deficiencies by partners, friends, family, and society in general. Within the communication differences, the dominant majority labels the differences as inferior, and ND communication styles are always seen as less valid. This is also seen in therapist's offices when NT partners try to paint a very clear picture of the deficiencies of their spouse and how "anyone" would "get" what the ND partner does not.

> *If you were dropped onto another planet, you would likely be traumatized. When an ND person lives in a neurotypical world, daily expectations can bring unmet expectations, social faux paus, and invalidation. It is not unusual for an ND person to suffer PTSD from traumas they have experienced from their own neurodiversity.*

To Diagnose or Not Diagnose?

ND: I've always felt so weird and alien to other people, and had come to terms with my weirdness. But to learn that it is because I truly process reality in a different way? My mind is blown. The fact that I now have a label for the odd things about myself has made my strangely more confident! So many things made sense, though, I just felt so validated! Now I'm learning to make my environment comfortable for me, instead of struggling in the existing one. Diagnosis is so important; if you don't know why you are experiencing certain things, and that it's part of a spe-

cific disorder, you won't be able to understand yourself, and your partner certainly won't be able to understand you.

NT: The diagnosis of my partner with Autism Spectrum has been helpful to some extent. It helped me understand that their behaviors were not necessarily deliberately meant to hurt me, but I still avoid going places with them so I don't have to explain their behavior.

The Centers for Disease Control currently estimates that 1 in 44 children are diagnosed on the autism spectrum, and that autism spectrum disorder is four times as common in boys as it is girls (CDC, 2020). And while this neurodiversity is more common in boys than girls, presently, there is awareness that how we assess typically lacks sensitivity to female traits of autism (Lai M-C, 2017). Women are harder to diagnose and often go under-diagnosed. Due to social expectations, they successfully mask, but at a cost to themselves in the energy spent to do this.

If you don't need accommodations at work or school, you may question the need for an assessment to ascertain a diagnosis of autism, ADHD, etc. This is certainly a personal decision to be made by each individual and couple. Typically, it is helpful to finally understand the "root" of some of the frustrating eccentricities and challenges that have become evident within the context of the relationship. Many people are getting diagnosed later in life and find it helps them finally make sense of many of their behaviors; partners can find it relieving to know why it feels that their partner lives on a different planet.

Female diagnosis of neurodiversity lags behind that of males in part due to complexity of how they present to the world. For example, Suckle (2020) notes that the behaviors that are often concealed that show evidence of autism include:

- Challenges to maintaining relationships over time (Lowry, 2017),

- Challenges in interacting in larger groups, but rather over relying on key friends (Kopp & Gillberg, 1992),
- Lack of understanding of power dynamics (which can lead to abusive friendships) (Cook, et al., 2018)
- Needing to control and dominate the rules of games (Hiller et al., 2014)
- Preoccupation with "setting up" and organizing games as opposed to spontaneous flexible play (Szalavitz, 2016)
- Some degree of social meltdowns/shutdowns (Hull, et al., 2017), and
- Possibly more severe phases of autistic burnout (Hull, et al., 2017, as cited in Suckle, 2020, p. 755).

Likewise, females with ADHD are underidentified and underdiagnosed, but share the common symptom of anxiety (Skogli, et al., (2013).

> *Many people find solace in getting a professional diagnosis of autism spectrum, ADHD, or other neurologically based disorders. It helps them make sense of their entire life and can be comforting. It is certainly helpful if they need accommodations in the workplace. This choice is up to you and whether it is advantageous to you in your daily life, work, or relationships.*

Mental Health Issues and the Neurotypical Partner

ND: My girlfriend has been super stressed and has recently gotten super pissed at me. I don't know how to calm her down and it's been a few days since she last talked to me.

I want to calm her down so we can still be together, but I don't know what to do.

NT: We are normally good together, but our fights are tough. I have PTSD and typically dissociate when we get into fights. I get very mean, and honestly unemotional. Then he shuts down, and I just ignore him for days.

NT partners, of course, experience their own mental-health issues, both separate from, and related to, living with an ND partner. As previously noted, there can be a level of burnout that occurs from the emotional labor involved in managing executive-function tasks that may fall to them. Unrelenting anger, loneliness, and frustration can all take a toll. NT partners need to feel supported and valued by their ND partner (and vice versa). NT partners need to address their own mental health needs and focus on feeling better themselves, and may need emotional support from outside of the relationship in order to thrive.

In my practice, I have noticed that many NT partners have initially found solace in the reliability, stoicism, and low emotionality of an ND partner. Over time, however, partners grow and change, and what was once rewarding becomes stunting as the NT person realizes the shortfalls to these characteristics with regard to the intimacy they need. Essentially, due to their own insecurity and/or traumatic background, the NT person chooses a partner who, by the way they are built, is unlikely to leave. However, the NT partner then becomes dissatisfied when their partner is satisfied with a relationship that does not feel very intimate to the NT partner. This can lead to a cycle of mistreatment where they say horrible things to their ND partner because they are confident the ND partner will not leave.

Conversely, another pattern is for a person who has low ego strength to match up with a smart ND person, who appears confident and driven. The NT individual will curtail their needs and are codependent with the ND person, and again, over time, resent focusing their life around the needs of another. As they begin to discover themselves, they must now start to navigate life with someone they have previously catered to and undo the codependence and establish healthier boundaries. This is not always met with a welcoming stance on the part of the partner, and conflict can begin to occur in a relationship that previously was sedate.

Chapter 9:

Who Is the Captain of this Ship? Power Issues in Neurodiverse Relationships

Like all relationships, power dynamics can manifest over the course of a relationship, and partners must figure out how to navigate these differences. Two common power issues arise from different sources. The first is "neurotypical imperialism," which is the idea that the neurotypical way of thinking and doing things is the "right" way. When an NT partner holds these beliefs, we hear things like "How can you not get this? Everyone else understands this!" The second power issue that can develop is when the ND partner manifests black-and-white thinking and is unable to see the perspective of their NT partner and believes they are "right." This leads to rounds of arguments where the ND acts like an attorney and presents their "case," while the NT partner either fights back from an emotional perspective or placates in order to get the issue to stop. Both of these power issues can be sources of frustration, and need to move to stances of listening and understand to move beyond them.

Neurotypical Imperialism

ND: My partner is always blaming me for something. He says "Other people understand this; why don't you?" It can be as simple as missing an appointment or forgetting something I said I would do for him, and he says things like "My friends don't understand why I stay with you."

NT: I highly suspect my boyfriend has undiagnosed autism spectrum disorder. He shuts down, stops communicating, is emotionally absent, is highly forgetful, and misses commitments. He seems to be in denial, and gets highly upset and defensive when I suggest there is something wrong with him. I was hoping he would be vulnerable and tell me what his challenges are.

Most people get defensive if you suggest there is something wrong with them. The issue for the purportedly NT partner is their needs aren't being met, but they cannot understand why their partner is hesitant to be vulnerable. The ND partner feels blamed, "less than," and the effect of this type of continued interaction is erosion of their self-esteem. In this example, we have a seemingly caring NT partner who has taken the stance of neurotypical imperialism.

When you are in the majority, it is easy to think you are right. What I have seen many times is a sort of neurotypical imperialism, where couples come in and the NT person wants to be proven right, that their partner is somehow defective, and all of the problems of the relationship somehow rest on their partner's shoulders. I hear things like:

- How can he forget my birthday?
- She was supposed to pick me up at work and totally blew it off!

It can be very frustrating for the NT person to live with the disabling aspects of their neurodiverse partner. They often feel like they are left spinning all of the plates in the air and are often exhausted, depleted and defeated. However, proving your partner is deficient is not going to solve the problem and amounts to what I call "neurotypical imperialism." Neurotypical imperialism is the belief that you are correct because "most people" agree with you about your view of the world. You and your partner have different brain styles, and that does not make them "wrong." It means that they are wired differently, and you no doubt fell in love with some of the things that unusual wiring brought to your relationship. It could be intelligence, talent, kindness, infallible memory, and so on; right now, you are probably looking at the downsides that come with having to live with the disabling portion of the neuro-diversity your partner has.

For the ND person, this can lead to getting caught in abusive relationships. They see the logic in the NT partner's arguments that they are deficient in social skills, giving the NT person credibility and power. If the NT person is kind and gentle, this goes well; if they approach it from an emotional imperialism perspective, it can feel they are "one-up" or superior. Furthermore, years of training in the school system growing up may have embedded this believe that there is something "wrong" with them, and so a part of the ND person may consciously or unconsciously agree with the imperialist beliefs. We are only just starting to understand ND brain styles, let alone appreciate them, so it is easy to have adapted to mainstream beliefs about "deficiencies" of neuro-divergent individuals.

Conversely, NT partners can be the ones who are "brow beaten" by the insistence of the ND person that they are right. ND people typically enjoy intellectual arguing and are able to engage in logical arguments for lengthy periods of time as it can be invigorating to them. This can cause a sense of defeat and hopelessness, anger, or resentment in the NT spouse.

Always Being Right

ND: I've developed an over-analytical, cautious, and weird approach with my partner (and others). I explain, make excuses, and am generally defensive and try to prove my point with my explanations.

NT: If I hear from my husband "that's not right," one more time, I will scream. He is constantly telling me I am wrong!

Many ND people are extraordinarily bright and have analytical minds. However, between having an analytical nature, focusing on logic, and difficulties seeing the perspective of others, they may insist they are right, putting their partner in the position of being "wrong." This typically creates friction between partners. A ND mind can get caught in the logic of things, and the person will explain to their partner consistently how "right" they are and how "wrong" their partner is. They even may sound like a lawyer presenting their case to the NT spouse. If the NT partner has poor ego strength, they may begin to believe that their partner is right and they are wrong. This, too, is a type of abusive relationship and can lead to a domineering partner who argues to infinity, and the NT partner, over time, may give in just to get some peace. The genesis of this is the black-and-white thinking issue, which is hard for some NDs to overcome without some outside intervention (therapy) to gain understanding. I have seen NT partners just "give up" on placating their partners rather than engage in a game of wits that they feel they can never win.

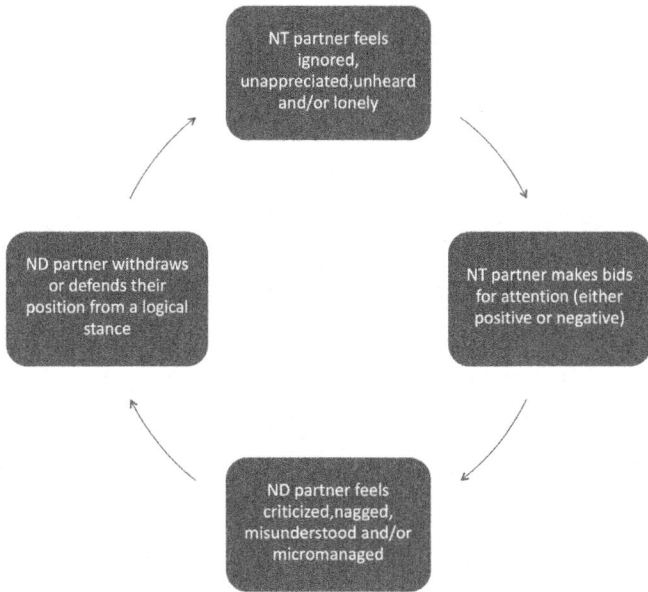

Figure 2.

This relational pattern (as seen in Figure 2) can lead to resentment by both partners. When the NT partner agrees to things they don't actually mean, and the ND partner trusts their NT partner is being authentic, a cascade of isolation and resentment can occur. If the ND partner finds that their partner has not been honest with them, trust is eroded, as they believed they and their partner were operating in good faith. The NT partner grows resentful at having to give in, placate, in order to "keep the peace" and end the monologuing.

A common complaint upon NT partners is the amount of arguing their ND partner can do, and they often comment about how they think their spouse actually enjoys arguing. There is a truthfulness in that, in that the ND partner does enjoy conversation that will bring about an objective truth. The problem is, in relationships, there are many areas where "truth" is not as important as feeling heard. The juxtaposition for the NT partner of "needing to be heard" versus the ND position of "getting to the truth" can leave partners at odds.

Chapter 10:

Close Encounters— The Voyage to Intimacy

ND: It is definitely about direct and open communication on both parts, otherwise there can be a lot of misunderstanding and resentment. I teach my partner how to respond to things, like if I am heading towards a meltdown and what she can do to assist. There is no reading between the lines for my wife. I have to be straight forward and to the point. If I'm upset and not very talkative, she won't notice unless I actually tell her "I am upset." It is definitely hard and testing at times.

NT: You may have to explain stuff that you don't have to explain to the average person. Be open about your feelings, because they may not understand how you feel without you being explicitly verbal and brutally honest. She's one of the only people who can be brutally honest with me, which is so refreshing, if a bit tactless at times. It's good to say exactly what you mean, being blunt and open is the best way to communicate.

Some of the disability portion of ND person may rear its head pretty consistently in everyday couple communication. The ND spouse may have trouble paying attention to what is said, be forgetful, or may experience meltdowns from sensory overload, with the NT partner sometimes the target for the emotional outburst. As partners begin to see each other differently, they can communicate in more productive ways. I talk with NT partners about being "kindly blunt." The ND partner needs things clearly spelled out, and will not take offense at the bluntness, but instead find it relieving. It will behoove an ND partner to take the advice of the March Hare in *Alice in Wonderland,* and "say what you mean," and "mean what you say." This will greatly help the ND partner understand what is wanted and needed, and decrease their strain of having to ferret out meaning in indirect or imprecise statements.

The Common Pattern in Neurodiverse Relationships

ND: The second my partner starts getting angry, I want to escape. It doesn't even matter if they are mad at me or not, I just want to escape. The "energy" coming off of them is overwhelming. I tend to immediately shut down if the anger is directed at me. I just want it to be over with. If they are giving me advice or explaining how I need to change my behavior, I can't process it until after the conflict is done and I am no longer in fight-or-flight mode.

NT: I get into the remind-remind-nag-nag mode. I feel like if I don't hound them about stuff, it doesn't get done. They get into the avoid-avoid-argue-argue mode. I'm so tired. But when I'm not angry, I love them. Love and hate are barely separated in my life! I love and adore my partner to death, and when they are having their good days, our relationship is nearly perfect, but when their symptoms are bad, it is such an uphill battle. I have my own issues too! I'm so angry and guilty, and I know they have real hindrances, but I am so tired!

Often due to the characteristics discussed in these pages, patterns in relationships develop. Most commonly, they are variations of an overfunctioner/underfunctioner pattern. So while the NT person may often overfunction, that can sometimes be reversed. For example, while the NT spouse may take care of daily tasks, the ND person may be especially good at financial management and take that over to the point the other person underfunctions in that area and knows little of family finances. Typically, however, the pattern that develops is based on how the couple handles daily mundane tasks that causes the difficulty.

The most common relational neurodiverse pattern typically looks like this:

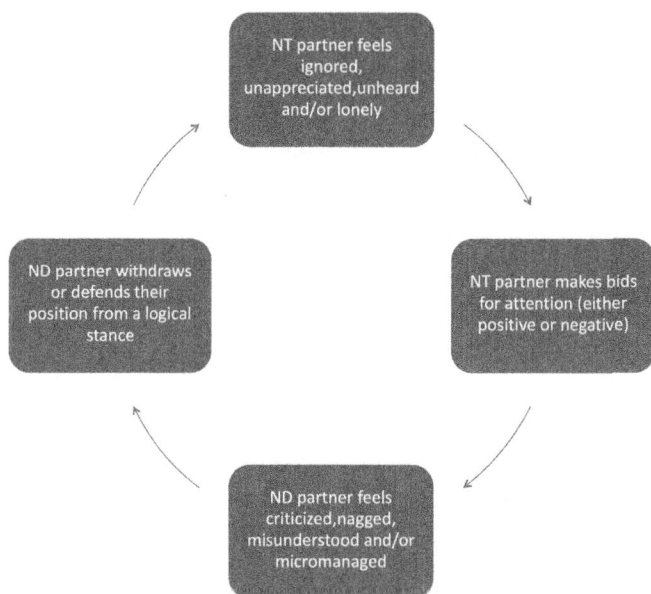

Figure 3.

As a relationship endures such as the one in Figure 3, patterns begin to emerge that frustrate the couple. Typically, this includes

119

the NT person feeling frustrated, angry or even rage-filled for having to manage daily life; they feel they are the "responsible one" in the relationship. They have been let down so many times by their partner, they have learned not to rely on their partner but are also bereft, feeling so lonely most every day. The NT partner has learned that if they ask for things, the ND partner does not reliably respond, and the NT partner resorts to ultimatums or demands in order to get results, leaving the NT partner feeling like they have to be the "bad guy" in order to get basic needs met. They may internalize when their partner cannot meet their needs that they do not care for them or love them.

The ND person often feels that their partner is always "on them," ready at the helm with criticism or nagging. They develop the belief that nothing they do will please their partner. They are essentially "damned if they do, and damned if they don't." They find themselves in the fight/flight/freeze mode often, and if they feel backed into a corner will often say things just to get their partner off their back. Sometimes they do not even remember saying these things because they are in fight/flight/freeze mode. Of course, when they make these promises and don't fulfill them, this increases the severity of the cycle. They may find their partner to be controlling; feeling micromanaged, they will resort to avoidance to deal with the feelings brought about by this pressure. They long for the days when they felt accepted and loved by their partner.

There is sometimes some distortion in this process as well because everyday tasks can be so draining for the ND person that, in their minds, their energy expenditure feels similar to their partner's so they do not see the discrepancy, which further aggravates their partner. The NT person may also have a hard time understanding how very difficult it is for their ND partner to do everyday tasks and exacerbate this cycle with their frustration and anger.

> *It is common for "demand-withdraw" patterns to develop in neurodiverse relationships. Typically, the NT partner sounds the alarm that their needs are not being met, and this is met with a shut down or withdrawal on the part of the ND partner. This causes the NT partner to get "louder" or more frequent with their demands, which causes further withdrawal and frustration. This pattern can get codified into the relationship and be frustrating for both partners.*

Gender and Orientation Diversity

ND: My partner and I are both on the spectrum. We've never had a problem with jealously and recently have gone from monogamy to polyamory. When I was on a date, my partner had a bit of a breakdown, not because of jealousy, but because they didn't know what to expect. We need to set some clear rules, but everything we find about rules in polyamory isn't very useful to us, because we don't communicate in a neurotypical way. For instance, I can talk about the concept of kissing people on a date, and then go on a date, but I need to talk about kissing that specific person on that specific date because my partner might otherwise not make the connection and be surprised that I kissed on the date even though I talked about it beforehand.

NT: My wife is on the autism spectrum, and has recently realized she is asexual. We still love each other, but we don't have sex anymore because we have crashed and burned too many times and now we both understand why.

121

We are talking about opening up our relationship and polyamory. I don't want her to get the short end of the stick, so we're talking about ground rules and compromises which will help us both get what we want and need without throwing away ten years of an otherwise loving and supportive partnership.

For ND individuals, particularly for those on the autism spectrum, there is evidence that there is increased nonheterosexuality (that is, there is increased homosexuality, bisexuality, and asexuality), as well as gender fluidity (George & Stokes, 2018). One study found that autistic adolescents and adults are about eight times more likely to consider themselves as "asexual" or "other orientations" than nonautistic individuals, and they are less likely to report sexually activity or heterosexuality compared to nonautistic individuals (Weir, Allison, & Baron-Cohen, 2021).

Partners should discuss parameters of their relationship. In some cases, there are less proscriptions against re-defining the type of relationship that works for the couple, which may include nontraditional relationships, or what Michaels and Johnson (2015) refer to as "designer relationships," which may include monogamy, polyamory, or open relationships.

For mixed relationships, when the ND partner approaches the relationship with less investment in the emotions related to fidelity, the NT partner can be confused and feel betrayed. Blunt communication about expectations regarding boundaries of the relationship is needed. Again, there are significant social rules around fidelity, monogamy, and gender that may need to be discussed. While these social rules are often assumed in neurotypical relationships, erring on the side of communication around these issues can lead to positive discussions about intimacy needs.

> *There typically is more gender and orientation diversity for those who are neurodiverse. Open couple communication around these topics is essential for navigation through them so both partners feel valued and safe within the context of the couple relationship.*

Substance Abuse

ND: I have ADHD, diagnosed as a child. ADHD is often paired with impulse control and I feel that was one of my challenges with alcohol use (binge drinker), coupled with the fact I have a diagnosis of generalized anxiety disorder (also common in ADHD) and I used alcohol to self-medicate for social anxiety. I self-medicated for 10 years, but now I am one week away from my two-year sobriety anniversary. It has been hard but it has been worth it.

NT: For a long time I rationalized my partner's drinking behaviors as a way to control her ADHD. She could work, and only drink in the evenings, so I thought it was okay. But the hurtful behaviors that occurred when she was drinking were not. I was oblivious and in love. Finally things came to a breaking point, and she got help for drinking, and I got help for my enabling behaviors. We're much better now, but it has taken a lot of work.

There is evidence that ADHD is associated with substance-abuse issues (Wilens, 2004), which often is an attempt to self-medicate. The research on autism finds some evidence of linkage to substance abuse, but the research is not conclusive at this point (Ressel, et. al., 2020). Substances as a way of coping with life can become be a problem for either partner. Typically, if it is the NT partner using substances, it is to cope with loneliness and isolation, or in some cases to deal with their own previous trauma. If it is the ND partner using substances, it typically has become a habituated way to deal with generalized anxiety or social anxiety. The question to ask is, "Do substances get in the way of me connecting with my partner?" However, connection is a two-way street, so you may answer this affirmatively, but your partner may not. It is important to pay attention to what your partner says about connection here. If *they* believe substances are getting in the way, you need to pay attention and look to other methods to cope with what is going on for you if you want your relationship to succeed and thrive. If both partners are using substances to cope with daily life, the question to answer would be "What would happen to us if we stop using substances?" Numbing to survive difficult relationships shortchanges both partners, as well as any children in the relationship.

> Substance abuse can appear for either the ND or NT partner as ways to cope with life stressors. ND partners may be coping with masking, executive functioning stressors, or social or generalized anxiety. NT partners may be coping with isolation or role overload.

Codependence

ND: Masking, or putting a lot of effort into appearing normal, causes me to be hyperaware and self-conscious. I have this constant internal commentary questioning myself with things like "What are they thinking? What is their face doing? What's the mood here? What do they want?" I feel like I have a hard time identifying what I am feeling because I am so focused on deciphering what they might be thinking.

NT: I spend every day trying to avoid landmines of what might set them off. I scurry to bring stuff up only when they are in a good space, avoiding anything that might displease them like the plague. I don't make morning appointments, because I can already hear the complaint "That's too early!" ringing in my ears. I always feel like I am hesitant or scared or walking on eggshells around them, not wanting to make them uncomfortable, as then there is hell to pay.

Codependence occurs when one person absorbs the feelings of another. While empathy is a great trait, when one is unable to untangle their own feelings from their partner, there can be an unhealthy codependence.

It is not unusual to find NTs who have a hard time with emotional autonomy paired with NDs. They are often naturally caring people and wish to help others. This trait becomes a problem, however, when the NT person cannot unhook from moods of the ND partner. For example, if an ND person has had a bad day, is moody and needs to distance to regain equilibrium, the NT person may take this personally. Martyrdom can develop when the NT partner believes they "do everything" for their partner with little reciprocity.

In the above example regarding masking, we can see that the person has developed a codependent stance because of their neurodiverse limitations that make it hard for them to read others. Again, if you are a stranger in a strange land, you will be hypersensitive to the natives in order to try to fit in for your own survival.

> *Codependence occurs in relationships when you put your energy into supporting others with less consideration for what you need for yourself. A person can disappear into the needs of the other person or be controlled by their needs rather than focusing on their own.*

Burnout in Neurodiverse Relationships. . . May I Get *Off* This Planet, Please?

The World Health Organization (2019) recently defined burnout as a diagnosable syndrome. It is not uncommon to see burnout in neurodiverse relationships for one or both partners. The burnout source is different, but the symptoms can be similar. Burnout out can be evidenced in physical, mental, and emotional exhaustion by either partner. There is no established research on burnout for partners of those who are ND and little on ND individuals themselves, with a minor exception for those on the autism spectrum. Yet, burnout is a real phenomenon and can greatly impact individuals and their relationships.

Burnout and the NT Partner

*NT: I am so exhausted all the time. I have to plan everything! I organize the house, pay the bills, do the majority of the housework, and work outside the home. My husband can't remember a thing, I organize all the kids' activities, I even am the one to remember to send a birthday present to **his** mother. And what do I get in return? It doesn't feel like much. I know he loves me, but some days it is all just too much.*

Spouses who bear the responsibility of many executive-functioning tasks (for example, planning, scheduling, organizing) can and do suffer burnout. There is research that helps us understand burnout in parents of autistic children (for example, Kütük, et al., 2021; Weiss, et al., 2014), but there is no available research to help us understand burnout for those in partnerships or marriages with ND persons. The closest literature we have to understand this phenomenon is research surrounding "informal caregivers."

Informal caregivers care for others facing illness, disabilities, or other conditions requiring attention (Gérain & Zech, 2019). These authors note that being an informal caregiver puts an individual at risk for poorer mental and physical health. Adapting the definition of burnout from the World Health Organization from the world of work and applying it to one's relationship, we might theorize that burnout for the NT partner may be due to executive-functioning overload that has not been successfully managed. It includes energy depletion or exhaustion, increased distance from one's relational partner or feelings of resentment or cynicism related to the relationship, and reduced efficacy in performing home and relational management tasks (Adapted from WHO, 2019).

Again, borrowing from caregiver research, we can begin to conceptualize what may occur for the NT partner. For caregivers there is a certain amount of burden, which is broken down into "objective" and "subjective" burden. The objective burden has to do with the actual time and energy it takes to do the caregiving. The subjective burden refers to how the caregiver perceives the burden of caring for their loved one (Flyckt, Fatouros-Bergman & Koernig, 2015). What I most commonly see with ND/NT relationships is that lack of understanding by the NT person of the ND partner's condition creates a dynamic whereby the NT person believes they are being deliberately emotionally deprived by the ND partner, and well deserved love is being withheld from them. In response to this perceived lack of love and affection, they become resentful when their needs are not being met. This then makes the tasks that they often take over, due to their partner's executive functioning and social challenges, more onerous. Over time, if these dynamics are not understood and dealt with, the NT partner may even experience psychosomatic symptoms such as headaches, muscle pain, sleep problems, nervousness, irritability, fatigue, and/or depression symptoms, which are common problems for caregivers in other situations, but this research has not yet been conducted for NT partners.

> *For the NT partner, burnout often is due to caregiver burdens brought on by the labor of doing much of the executive functioning tasks, feeling emotionally deprived, and simmering resentments may occur as they believe they have a larger burden within the home.*

Burnout and the ND Partner

ND: For me, I think autistic burnout is when I am low on emotional energy, and my sensory issues are intensified. I don't want to speak, I don't want to make eye contact, I don't want any sensory input. I'm also not able to express any positive feeling in NT ways (smiling, laughing). I find myself crying more, stimming, and sleeping more, and being unable to mask.

Burnout for the ND partner is often a response to living in a neurotypical world and having to mask ND traits. Again, we do not have much research on this topic except for a few articles on autistic burnout (for example, Raymaker, et al., 2020). It may be accompanied by physical or emotional exhaustion, including symptoms of depression, anger, and anxiety. The ND individual may see increased sensory sensitivities. The outside world may see indicators such as irritability, withdrawal, increased sensory issues, stimming, and repetitive behavior. Executive functioning, impulse control, cognitive skills, and short term memory may become impaired.

Raymaker, et al. (2020) are the first to empirically explore autistic burnout in their article aptly named: "'Having All of Your Internal Resources Exhausted Beyond Measure and Being Left With No Cleanup Crew': Defining Autistic Burnout." Gathering qualitative information from interviews and other sources, they found the following things experienced during burnout:

- Chronic life stress
- Mismatch of expectations by others and their own abilities
- Inadequate support
- Long-term exhaustion (typically 3+ months)
- Loss of function
- Reduced tolerance to stimulus

Raymaker and colleagues posit that life stressors such as masking, family and societal expectations (including school and work), managing the disability aspects of autistic differences in often nonaccomodating environments, as well as life changes and transitions can all negatively impact the autistic adult (2020). When these factors are coupled with barriers to support such as experiencing gaslighting or dismissing of their symptoms, poor boundaries, poor self-advocacy skills, inability to take a break, and a lack of external resources and support, they note that for the autistic adult expectations outweigh abilities and burnout ensues. It is likely this process is similar for other ND adults.

> For ND individuals, burnout is likely
> to be experienced when stressors
> outweigh one's ability to obtain relief
> and expectations outweigh abilities.

Disenfranchised Grief

NT: In the end, we love each other, but I miss feeling connected to my partner. I think the hardest thing is their lack of ability to see my perspective and understand my feelings. It makes me feel isolated and disconnected.

ND: Sometimes I don't think my partner understands me because we are so fundamentally different. Don't get me wrong, I feel lucky to have them, but it is so hard because I have no idea what needs I have and how to communicate that. And they get so frustrated when I can't communicate! It feels like they are constantly mad at me, and I often hear "You just don't get it!"

NT partners often experience grief when they realize they will never have the marriage they envisioned with their partner. Grief becomes disenfranchised when society does not support it, and many NT partners have spouses who look to the outside world like ideal mates, so others may question why they are suffering within the marriage/relationship, or they may doubt the validity of their suffering. The loss that NT partners experience occurs when there is a realization about the loss of the type of intimacy they were hoping to have in their relationship. This is a loss of what was hoped for in the marriage, what could have been, and what the relationship actually is. Sometimes it is easier to assume the ND person is deliberately refusing to change rather than accept this reality.

The ND partner can face a different kind of grief that is equally disenfranchised. They mourn the loss of a relationship where they initially felt accepted and loved. They miss the partnership they once had, the appreciation they garnered from their partner for their own native talents, and the calm of that time. There can be a loss of feeling comfortable in your own home when it gets reinforced that you are not meeting the needs of others around you.

> *Both partners can experience disenfranchised grief as their expectations for what they wanted in a partnership bear little resemblance to reality, and their needs for being cared for, heard and accepted are not met.*

Why Join Orbits?

ND: My wife is NT, I'm an aspie. I actually never dated until I met my wife and I was 27 when we met. We have our struggles and some days are harder than others. We try to keep things open and honest between each other, so neither is overwhelmed or feels ignored. I didn't think I would ever get married or even date, but here we are. It is very nice to have someone to help me tackle things that need to be done and keep me on track. It also helps that I can be completely honest with her and just be myself and not have to mask or be something other than myself.

NT: My partner, who is on the autism spectrum, loves fiercely, is very loyal and protective. He has his quirks, gets focused on topics and often talks about it for ages. Absolutely hates change, but loves to problem-solve. Life is not easy when the world is at direct odds with how your whole brain is wired!

The strengths that NDs bring to the table are many. And while it sometimes looks like they are less sensitive, the reality is that your ND partner is sensitive to the point where it causes them significant distress. I'm not sure about you, but I think the world could do with more sensitivity, not less. What we often find in ND partners are people who are reliable, committed, and significantly talented in at least one area of life. They see the world differently, and this intrigued you. Your partner may also be a great problem-solver, great with numbers, trustworthy, creative, and so on. You chose an interplanetary relationship, and can expect surprises and delights as well as some alien traits that are hard to understand.

For the ND partner, they can thrive when they have the support of a loving partner who understands their different abilities and can respect that there are some areas in life that are unusually challenging, often driven by sensory issues or executive functioning problems. The ND brings a different lens to life that can enliven both partners once it is understood and accepted. Who wouldn't want to visit another planet and learn how its inhabitants think, feel, and behave?

> *A neurodiverse relationship is a cross-cultural relationship. You can learn so much from each other, and as you embrace your diverse brain styles, you can appreciate the trip through the universe of your relationship.*

Resources

Books

Attwood, T. (2007). *The Complete Guide to Asperger's Syndrome.* London: Jessica Kingsley Publishers.

Bédard, R. & Hecker, L. (Eds.) (2020). *A Spectrum of Solutions for Clients With Autism: Treatment for Adolescents and Adults.* New York: Routledge Press.

Cook, B., & Garnett, M. (Eds.) (2018). *Spectrum Women: Walking to the Beat of Autism.* London: Jessica Kingsley Publishers.

Gaus, V. (2011). *Living Well on the Spectrum: How to Use Your Strengths to Meet the Challenges of Asperger Syndrome/High-Functioning Autism.* New York: Guilford Press.

O'Toole, J. C. (2018). *Autism in Heels.* New York: Skyhorse.

Robison, J. E. (2012). *Be Different: My Adventures with Asperger's and My Advice for Fellow Aspergians, Misfits, Families, and Teachers.* New York: Crown Publishing.

Robison, J. E. (2009). *Look Me In the Eye: My Life with Asperger's.* London: Ebury.

Toksvig, S. (2015). *The Tricky Art of Co-Existing: How to Behave Decently No Matter What Life Throws Your Way.* New York: The Experiment.

Websites

Asperger/Autism Network (AANE), AANE.org

Autism Society of America, AutismSociety.org

Indiana Resource Center for Autism, iidc.indiana.edu/irca

Orange County Asperger's Support Group, OCAspergers.org

Spectrum Women, SpectrumWomen.com

Temple Grandin, TempleGrandin.com

Yellow Ladybugs, YellowLadybugs.com.au

References

American Psychiatric Association. (2013). *Diagnostic and statistical manual of mental disorders* (5th ed.). doi.org/10.1176/appi.books.9780890425596

Anonymously Autistic. (2016). The anguish of brushing your teeth when you have sensory issues. The Mighty. TheMighty.com/2016/11/what-brushing-your-teeth-is-like-when-you-have-sensory-issues

Ashinoff, B. K., Abu-Akel, A. (2019). Hyperfocus: the forgotten frontier of attention. *Psychological Research, 85*, 1–19. doi.org/10.1007/s00426-019-01245-8

Ashwin, C., Chapman, E., Howells, J., et al. Enhanced olfactory sensitivity in autism spectrum conditions (2014). *Molecular Autism, 5*, 53. doi.org/10.1186/2040-2392-5-53

Astington, J. W. & Edward, M. J. (2017). The development of theory of mind in early childhood. *Encyclopedia of Early Childhood Development*, pp. 1–37. doc.uments.com/s-the-development-of-theory-of-mind-in-early-childhood.pdf

Bermond, B., Clayton, K., Liberova, A., Luminet, O., Maruszewski, T., Bitti, P. E. R., Rimé, B.,Vorst, H. H., Wagner, H. & Wicherts, J. (2007). A cognitive and affective dimensions of alexithymia in six languages and seven populations. *Cognition and Emotion, 21*(5), 1125–1136

Bertilsdotter Rosqvist, H., Jackson-Perry, D. (2021). Not doing it properly? (Re)producing and resisting knowledge through narratives of autistic sexualities. *Sex and Disability, 39*, 327–344. doi.org/10.1007/s11195-020-09624-5

Boucher, J., & Bowler, D. (Eds.). (2008). *Memory in Autism: Theory and evidence.* Cambridge: Cambridge University Press.

Caruana, N., Stieglitz Ham, H., Brock, J., Woolgar, A., Kloth, N., Palermo, R., McArthur, G. (2018, May). Joint attention difficulties in autistic adults: An interactive eye-tracking study. *Autism, 22*(4):502–512. doi: 10.1177/1362361316676204. Epub 2017 Apr 20. PMID: 28423919

Cassidy, S., Bradley, L., Shaw, R., Baron-Cohen, S. (2018). Risk markers for suicidality in autistic adults. *Molecular Autism, 9*(42):1–14. doi.org/10.1186/s13229-018-0226-4

CDC (2020, Sept. 25). Data & statistics on autism spectrum disorder. CDC.gov/ncbddd/autism/data.html

Center for Creative Leadership. (2021). Adapting to change requires flexible leadership. CCL.org/articles/leading-effectively-articles/adaptability-1-idea-3-facts-5-tips

CHADD. (2019, July 19). When depression co-occurs with ADHD. chadd.org/adhd-weekly/when-depression-co-occurs-with-adhd

Christopher, G., & McDonald, J. (2005). The impact of clinical depression on working memory. *Cognitive Neuropsychiatry, 10*, 379–399. doi: 10.1080/13546800444000128

Cook, A., Ogden, J., & Winstone, N. (2018). Friendship motivations, challenges and the role of masking for girls with autism in contrasting school settings. *European Journal of Special Needs Education, 33*(3), 302–315. doi.org/10.1080/08856257.2017.1312797

Coulter, R. A. (2009). Understanding the visual symptoms of individuals with Autism Spectrum Disorder (ASD). *Optometry and Vision Development, 40*(3), 164–175.

Craig A. D. (2015). How do you feel? An interoceptive moment with your neurobiological self. New Jersey: Princeton University Press; 10.1515/9781400852727.

Crane, L., Goddard, L., & Pring, L. (2009). Sensory processing in adults with autism spectrum disorders. *Autism, 13*(3), 215–228. doi.org/10.1177/1362361309103794

Edelstein, M., Brang, D., Rouw, R., & Ramachanan, V. S. (2013). Misophonia: physiological investigations and case descriptions. *Frontiers in Human Neuroscience, 7*, 296. FrontiersIn.org/articles/10.3389/fnhum.2013.00296/full

Flyckt, L., Fatouros-Bergman, H., & Koernig, T. (2015). Determinants of subjective and objective burden of informal caregiving of patients with psychotic disorders. *The International Journal of Social Psychiatry, 61*(7), 684–692. doi.org/10.1177/0020764015573088

Gamin, A., Godin, O., Scheid, I., Monnet, D., Murzi, E., Teruel, A.M., Amsellem, F, Laouamri, H., Souyris, K., Houneau, J, & Infor, T. (2017). Psychiatric co-morbidities in a French cohort of adults with high-functioning autism (HFA). *European Psychiatry, 41*, S136.

George, R., & Stokes, M. A. (2018). Sexual orientation in Autism Spectrum Disorder. *Autism Research: Official Journal of the International Society for Autism Research, 11*(1), 133–141. doi.org/10.1002/aur.1892

Gérain, P. & Zech, E. (2019) Informal caregiver burnout? Development of a theoretical framework to understand the impact of caregiving. *Frontiers in Psychology, 10*:1748. doi: 10.3389/fpsyg.2019.01748.

Gernsbacher, M. A., & Yergeau, M. (2019). Empirical failures of the claim that autistic people lack a theory of mind. *Archives of Scientific Psychology, 7*(1), 102–118. doi: 10.1037/arc0000067.

Gottman, J., & DeClaire, J. (2004). *The relationship cure.* New York: Random House.

Gottman, J., & Silver, N. (2015) *The seven principles for making marriage work.* (rev. ed.) New York: Three Rivers.

Grandin, T. (2020) *Different. . . not less: Inspiring stories of achievement and successful employment from adults with Autism, Asperger's, and ADHD.* (2nd ed.) Texas: Future Horizons.

Harris, Z. (n.d.) Beating time blindness. CHADD. chadd.org/attention-article/beating-time-blindness

Hartley, G. (2018). *Fed up: Emotional labor, women, and the way forward.* New York: Harper One.

Hiller, R. M., Young, R. L., & Weber, N. (2014). Sex differences in Autism Spectrum Disorder based on DSM-5 criteria: Evidence from clinician and teacher reporting. *Journal of Abnormal Child Psychology, 42*(8), 1381–1393. doi.org/10.1007/s10802-014-9881-x

Hofvander, B., Delorme, R., Chaste, P., Nydén, A., Wentz, E., Ståhlberg, O., . . . & Råstam, M. (2009). Psychiatric and psychosocial problems in adults with normal-intelligence autism spectrum disorders. BMC *Psychiatry, 9,* 35. doi.org/10.1186/1471-244X-9-35

Hull, L., Petrides, K. V., Allison, C., Smith, P., Baron-Cohen, S., Lai, M.-C., et al. (2017). "Putting on my best normal": Social camouflaging in adults with Autism Spectrum conditions. *Journal of Autism and Developmental Disorders, 47,* 2519. doi.org/10.1007/s10803-017-3166-5

Kessler, R. C., Adler, L., Barkley, R., et al. (2006). The prevalence and correlates of adult ADHD in the United States: Results from the national comorbidity survey replication. *American Journal of Psychiatry, 163*(4):716–723. doi:10.1176/ajp.2006. 163.4.716

Kopp, S., & Gillberg, C. (1992). Girls with social deficits and learning problems: Autism, atypical Asperger syndrome of a variant of these conditions. *European Child & Adolescent Psychiatry, 1*(2), 89–99. doi.org/10.1007/BF02091791

Kütük, M.Ö., Tufan, A. E., Kılıçaslan, F., Güler, G., Çelik, F., Altınta, E., Gökçen, C., Karada , M., Yekta , Ç., Mutluer, T., Kandemir, H., Büber, A., Topal, Z., Acikbas, U., Giray, A., & Kütük, Ö. (2021). High depression symptoms and burnout levels among parents of children with Autism Spectrum Disorders: A multi-center, cross-sectional, case–control study. *Journal of Autism and Developmental Disorders, 51*(11), 4086–4099. doi.org/10.1007/s10803-021-04874-4.

Lane, S. J., Miller, L. J. & Hanft, B. E. (2000). Toward a consensus in terminology in sensory integration theory and practice: Part 2: Sensory integration patterns of function and dysfunction. *Sensory Integration Special Internet Section Quarterly, 23*, 1–3.

Lowry, L. (2017). Misunderstood girls: A look at gender differences in autism. Hanen Early Language Program. hanen.org/ SiteAssets/Articles---Printer-Friendly/Research-in-your-Daily-Work/Misunderstood-Girls-A-look-at-gender-differences-i. aspx

Lugnegård, T., Hallerbäck, M. U., & Gillberg, C. (2011). Psychiatric comorbidity in young adults with a clinical diagnosis of Asperger syndrome. *Research in Developmental Disabilities, 32*, 1910–1917. doi.org/10.1016/j.ridd.2011.03.025.

Mandy, W. & Lai, M. C, (2017). Towards sex and gender informed autism research. *Autism, 21*(6), 643–645. doi: 10. 1177/1362361317706904

McMahon, K., Anand, D., Morris-Jones, M., & Rosenthal, M. Z. (2019). A path from childhood sensory processing disorder to anxiety disorders: The mediating role of emotion dysregulation and adult sensory processing disorder symptoms. *Frontiers in Integrative Neuroscience, 13*, 22–22. doi.org/10.3389/fnint.2019.00022

Michaels, M. A. & Johnson, P. J. (2015). *Designer relationships: A guide to happy monogamy, positive polyamory, and optimistic open relationships.* New Jersey: Cleis Press.

Ocak, E., Eshraghi, R. S., Danesh, A., Mittal, R., & Eshraghi, A. A. (2018). Central auditory processing disorders in individuals with Autism Spectrum Disorders. *Balkan Medical Journal, 35*(5), 367–372. doi.org/10.4274/balkanmedj.2018. 0853

Rabiee, A., Vasaghi-Gharamaleki, B., Samadi, S. A., Amiri-Shavaki, Y., & Alaghband-Rad, J. (2020). Working memory deficits and its relationship to Autism Spectrum Disorders. *Iranian Journal of Medical Sciences, 45*(2), 100–109. doi.org/10.30476/IJMS.2019.45315

Raymaker, D. M., Teo, A. R., Stickler, N. A., Lentz, B., Scharer, M., Santos, A. D., Kapp, S. K., Hunter, M., Joyce, A., & Nicolaidis, C. (2020). "Having all of your internal resources exhausted beyond measure and being left with no cleanup crew": Defining autistic burnout. *Autism in Adulthood, 2*(2), 132-143. doi.org/10.1089/aut.2019.0079

Ressel, M., Thompson, B., Poulin, M-H., Normand, C.L., Fisher, M.H, Couture, G, & Iarocci, G. (2020). Systematic review of risk and protective factors associated with substance use and abuse in individuals with Autism Spectrum Disorders. *Autism: The International Journal of Research and Practice, 24*(4), 899-918. doi.org/10.1177/1362361320910963

Rumball, F. A. (2019). A systematic review of the assessment and treatment of Posttraumatic Stress Disorder in individuals with Autism Spectrum Disorders. *Review Journal of Autism and Developmental Disorders, 6*, 294–324. doi.org/10.1007/s40489-018-0133-9

Schauder, K. B., & Bennetto, L. (2016). Toward an interdisciplinary understanding of sensory dysfunction in Autism Spectrum Disorder: An integration of the neural and symptom literatures. *Frontiers in Neuroscience, 10*, 268. doi.org/10.3389/fnins.2016.00268

Singer, J. (2017). *NeuroDiversity: The birth of an idea.* Amazon Digital Services.

Skodzik T, Holling H, Pedersen A. (2017). Long-term memory performance in adult ADHD. *Journal of Attention Disorders, 21*(4):267-283. doi: 10.1177/1087054713510561.

Skogli, E. W., Teicher, M. H., Andersen, P. N., Hovik, K. T., & Øie, M. (2013). ADHD in girls and boys—gender differences in co-existing symptoms and executive function measures. *BMC Psychiatry, 13*, 298. doi.org/10.1186/1471-244X-13-298

Spencer, A. E., Faraone, S. V., Bogucki, O. E., Pope, A. L., Uchida, M., Milad, M. R., Spencer, T. J., Woodworth, K. Y., & Biederman, J. (2016). Examining the association between Posttraumatic Stress Disorder and Attention-Deficit/Hyperactivity Disorder: A systematic review and meta-analysis. *The Journal of Clinical Psychiatry, 77*(1), 72–83. doi.org/10.4088/JCP.14r09479

Suckle, E. K. DSM-5 and challenges to female autism identification. *Journal of Autism and Developmental Disorders, 51,* 754–759 (2021). doi.org/10.1007/s10803-020-04574-5

Szalavitz, M. (2016). Autism—It's different in girls. *Scientific American.* ScientificAmerican.com/article/autism-it-s-different-in-girls

Ward, M. F., Wender, P. H., & Reimherr, F. W. (1993). The Wender Utah Rating Scale: An aid in the retrospective diagnosis of childhood Attention Deficit Hyperactivity Disorder. *The American Journal of Psychiatry, 150*(6), 885–890. doi.org/10.1176/ajp.150.6.885

Weir, E., Allison, C., & Baron-Cohen, S. (2021). The sexual health, orientation, and activity of autistic adolescents and adults. *Autism Research,* 1–13. doi.org/10.1002/aur.2604.

Weiss, J. A., Wingsiong, A., & Lunsky, Y. (2014). Defining crisis in families of individuals with autism spectrum disorders. *Autism : The International Journal of Research and Practice, 18*(8), 985–995. doi.org/10.1177/1362361313508024.

White, S. W., Bray, B. C. & Ollendick, T. H. (2012). Examining shared and unique aspects of social anxiety disorder and Autism Spectrum Disorder using factor analysis. *Journal of Autism and Developmental Disorders, 42,* 874–884. doi.org/10.1007/s10803-011-1325-7

WHO (28 May, 2019). Burn-out an "occupational phenomenon": International classification of diseases. who.int/news/item/28-05-2019-burn-out-an-occupational-phenomenon-international-classification-of-diseases

Wilbarger, P., & Wilbarger, J. L. (1991). *Sensory defensiveness in children aged 2-12: An intervention guide for parents and other caretakers.* Santa Barbara, CA: Avanti Educational Programs.

Wilens, T. E. (2004). Impact of ADHD and its treatment on substance abuse in adults. *Journal of Clinical Psychiatry, 65* (3), 38–45. PMID: 15046534.

Acknowledgements

This book would not have been written without much assistance. I want to first acknowledge the many neurodivergent people who have poured their hearts out and have taught us neurotypicals how to better understand their internal worlds. This is certainly not their responsibility, but I am grateful for what I have learned. To me, neurodivergent folks light the world with intelligence, creativity, humor, and soul. I would like to thank Rachel Magario for her initial help organizing this project and cheerleading me to the finish line. She is so incredibly gifted in so many areas that I am in constant awe of her abilities. I am indebted to Dylan Lee, my intern for this project who helped with technical details and some personal insights and was reliable, fun, hard-working and immensely talented. He also designed this book cover. I wish to thank the Division of Vocational Resources for funding him with hopes that this internship will land him the technology job he really desires and can do so incredibly well. I want to thank Dr. Rachel Bédard for her unwavering support for my professional interests, her desire to help, her proofreading, and for just being one of the best people I have ever had the opportunity to know who betters the lives of others, especially those with autism. My friend all the way back from High School at Pearl City, Illinois, Alan Iandola, lent me the idea of "neurotypical imperialism," and I am forever grateful for his encouragement. As a copy editor, my new friend Kathleen Attridge was both grammatically astute, stuck to deadline, and very supportive of this project. A shout out to Cyndi Guesel for her belief in me during the early planning of this project, our "allowing times," and her sunny attitude about life's opportunities and challenges. To Shawn Shiraz for late night talks and drinks to keep me sane, I say "cheers." My long term friend, Anna Bower, needs a big thanks for always checking in on me. And lastly, a very special thanks goes to Dave Arns, for helping whip both this book and my spiritual life into production.

Nearly all of these folks orbit in the world of neurodiversity and shine bright lights for the futures of others. I am so deeply impressed with my neurodivergent daughter, Erin Schlossberger, who has more courage and heart than anyone else I know in this life. She has taught me much. And thank you to my brilliant son, Noah Schlossberger, who fixes things for me and cheers me on, all while studying quantum physics and climbing boulders. I am truly blessed. Lastly, thank you, dear reader, for learning more about this important topic! May this book help your orbits join, and there be peace on your part of earth.

About the Author

Lorna Hecker is a Professor Emerita from Purdue University Northwest, where she taught family therapy for 25 years, and directed the university's Couple and Family Therapy Center. She is a coach for neurodiverse individuals and couples. She maintains the Center for Neurodiverse Wellness in Fort Collins, Colorado, where she also operates a private practice as a licensed marriage and family therapist. She has written or edited ten mental health related books, including *A Spectrum of Solutions for Clients with Autism: Treatment for Adolescents and Adults* (co edited with Dr. Rachel Bédard). You can find her at the Center for Neurodiverse Wellness at www.NeurodiverseWellness.com or HeckerCounseling.com.

Printed in Great Britain
by Amazon

49128514R00086